CRUMBS OF COMFORT

Books by Minnie M. Dalton

Crumbs of Comfort

Bread on the Waters

Every Day Living

Heaven and Earth

Sidewalks of Life

CRUMBS OF COMFORT

Poems by
Minnie M. Dalton

Exposition Press   *New York*

EXPOSITION PRESS, INC.

50 Jericho Turnpike, Jericho, New York 11753

FIRST EDITION

SBN 0-682-47654-4

I dedicate this book with love
To people who have older grown;
A brave, older generation,
Their faith and loyalty they have shown.

Through their many years of service
Hardship, disappointments were there,
A brave, older generation
Has been ready, their gifts to share.

They built a nation with ideals,
Patriotism, steadfast and true,
Paved a road of honesty
That is always good to renew.

I dedicate this book with love,
To people who have older grown,
A brave, older gerenation
That the younger people have known.

CONTENTS

CRUMBS OF COMFORT

CRUMBS OF COMFORT

Little crumbs on the sea—
Trying hard to be free,
Forgotten are their cares—
Will someday think of thee.

Little crumbs ride the waves,
Hear the sounds from the deep;
Beneath the restless waves
Are loved ones asleep?

Little crumbs, listen well,
There is something to hear,
There is a whisper sweet,
Bring it to someone dear.

Little crumbs on the sea
Trying hard to be free,
Music comes from the deep,
Crumbs of comfort for thee.

A SMILE

A smile begets a smile.
These words are very true;
Greet someone with a smile,
Then a smile will greet you.

A smile begets a smile
And drives a frown away;
No one can be angry,
Face a smile bright and gay.

A smile begets a smile,
A word gentle and sweet
Will make a better world,
A happy day complete.

A smile begets a smile;
These words are very true.
Meet the world with a smile,
Then a smile will meet you.

THANKSGIVING

Be ye thankful unto the Lord
For blessings on Thanksgiving Day;
Choose the things that bring happiness
For home and friends, children at play.

Be ye thankful unto the Lord
For work to do and gentle touch,
For the Spirit of love and peace,
That a hungry world needs so much.

Be ye thankful unto the Lord,
Give to God the glory today,
In humility seek His Love,
Never let thy heart go astray.

Be ye thankful unto the Lord,
Friendship and fellowship to know,
Cast thy bread upon the waters,
Find quiet peace love can bestow.

CRUMBS OF COMFORT

Look for the crumbs of comfort
That are in every day of life,
There are always some to be found,
Though the world be full of strife.

Look for the crumbs of comfort,
There will be little crumbs of love,
They are always found somewhere,
Innocent as a little dove.

Look for the crumbs of comfort,
Symbols of goodness and truth,
To comfort the little ones,
The young, aged and the youth.

Look for the crumbs of comfort,
Though little things they may be,
The world is a better place,
Nearer to eternity.

AUTUMN LEAVES

Autumn leaves sing a lullaby.
When they are falling to the ground,
A quiet world will go to sleep
To the gentle musical sound.

Autumn leaves sing a lullaby,
While they blanket the earth in brown,
Patiently the animals all wait
While leaves blanket country and town.

Autumn leaves sing a lullaby
To Nature's children in the fall,
They dream dreams of the coming spring,
Plan to be ready for Springtime's call.

Autumn leaves sing a lullaby,
Little seeds are where they belong,
Their world will live and grow again,
When it is time for Springtime's song.

CRUMBS OF COMFORT

Crumbs of comfort will keep in touch
With the dear ones they love so much,
Always near and ready to see,
To fill a need and comfort be.

Forgiving love and tender grace,
To heal a hurt in any place,
Forget the cost—generous be—
For love itself sets the world free.

No interest or notes are made,
Love can accept, be unafraid.
No stormy waves but life is calm,
Love forever, a healing balm.

Crumbs of comfort will keep in touch,
Strong with love they will need no crutch,
True to their ideals, makes them strong,
They always stay where they belong.

CREATIVE WORK

Creative work is just as good,
Thought it may never win a prize.
Lovely dreams that came from the heart,
Are being seen through other eyes.

Creative work is bravely done,
The storms of life have taken toll,
Through it all comes beauty, for it
Expresses Heaven in the soul.

Creative work always goes on,
The builders of the ages say.
Something beautiful left behind,
A witness to the world each day,

Creative work is just as good
As when people appreciate,
In the beginning there was God,
That gave talent and made it great.

BIRTHDAY

Give thanks unto the Lord,
For another birthday,
The Eternal Light shines
To light a future day.

Give thanks unto the Lord,
People have much to learn;
God is the only answer
He shows the way to turn.

Give thanks unto the Lord,
Remember all the past,
There will be something good
That will forever last.

Give thanks unto the Lord,
For the good and the just,
Birthdays Belong to God,
And He will keep His trust.

ONE LITTLE KISS

One little kiss from a child,
Blessed reward for the years
That are spent in loving care,
While healing its hurts and tears.

One little kiss from a child,
Memories that it creates,
The gentle comforting touch
Lifts the soul and elevates.

One little kiss from a child
Given in response to love,
Makes Heaven seem much closer,
Lifts the soul to heights above.

One little kiss from a child,
A loving blessed reward,
Life will always be richer,
Now, forever afterward.

GREATEST POWER

The unseen hand of God,
The greatest power on earth,
It gives strength to the soul,
Through grace and the new birth.

The world can never see,
Why Christians are so strong,
The unseen hand of God,
Keeps them where they belong.

Temptations are around,
A troubled world can see,
There will never be peace,
Until their souls are free.

The unseen hand of God,
The greatest help to know,
The road is clear and straight,
Another world to know.

WEAR A SMILE

The loneliest place in all the world
Is on a crowded city street,
When the tramping feet hurry by,
No friendly faces there to greet.

A thousand things are calling out,
The world can see no foe or friend,
Self-centered, the people seek
Something to make their troubles end.

Friendliness should begin at home,
To make new paths for tramping feet,
The light of faith should be planted,
A better world made complete.

The loneliest place in all the world
Is on a crowded city street,
Do think awhile and wear a smile
For the next person that you meet.

FAITH

Crumbs of faith can a comfort be,
Sailing life's tempestuous sea,
Bread on the waters, clear and pure,
Willing and ready to reassure.

Homeward bound in the way of truth,
Life-giving strength to age and youth,
The way narrow, the road straight,
Blessings come to the ones who wait.

Crumbs of faith that will fill a need,
Above the world, troubles and greed,
Ready to live and to believe,
Open hearts ready to receive.

Homeward bound through the ties of love,
See the stars and Heaven above;
Faith to believe, faith to be brave,
God's love can reach the soul to save.

LOVE

Love is often a fleeting thing,
Like a bird with a broken wing,
With a broken heart and alone,
No resting place, no cornerstone.

Love is often a fleeting thing,
With dreams and hopes, trying to cling,
That looks for moments that will bless,
To fulfill dreams, bring happiness.

Love is often a fleeting thing,
Its tender melodies to sing,
In after years it often gleams
Like sunny days in sunshine dreams.

Love is often a fleeting thing,
Memories it will often bring,
Gleaming gold in a crystal stream,
A summer night's pale moonlight beam.

CRUMBS OF COMFORT

Think awhile and wear a smile,
Crumbs of comfort will be there
When days are fair, then prepare,
The sunshine will go somewhere.

See a need, then do a deed,
Time has gone but love lives on,
Do not cry or even sigh,
Let the heart kindness enthrone.

Go forth with zest, do the best,
Then all the world surely knows,
No regrets or grief besets
Over stormy wind that blows.

Think awhile, and wear a smile,
Crumbs of comfort will be there,
Onward do good to bestow
Sunshine of hope to share.

BOOK OF TIME

There will always be problems
That belong to youth and age,
Generations create their own,
The Book of Time adds each page.

The old criticize the youth,
The youth criticize the old,
And neither has the answer,
The answers have not been told.

The old have brought their problems,
To carry along with them,
Where youth will plant seedlings
From which new problems stem.

There will always be new problems
That belong to youth and age,
Youth and age, understanding
The Book of Times adds a clean page.

GOD CAN GUIDE AMERICA

Come back, ye little children,
That we knew in yesteryear,
Pledge allegiance to our Flag,
The land that we hold dear.

Remember the Stars and Stripes,
The country for which it stands,
Respected around the world,
Mercy and Justice demands.

Under God indivisible,
It will reach a higher state,
Where all the little children
Remember to elevate.

Come back, ye little children,
That we knew in yesteryear,
God can guide America,
There will be nothing to fear.

CLOSE TO HEAVEN

Babies are close to Heaven
Where guardian angels live;
The babies listen and smile,
While they all their blessings give.

Babies are close to Heaven,
Mothers sing a lullaby,
The little stars twinkle,
With happiness from the sky.

Babies are close to Heaven,
They can hear the angels sing,
They carry back the message,
Happy smiles to earth they bring.

Babies are close to Heaven,
Their parents know this is true;
Little babies smile and love,
Each baby a blessing new.

MISSISSIPPI

The mighty Mississippi
In its greatness still and deep,
In its mighty strength moves on,
With all its secrets keep.

It knows so much history,
Time will always sing its song,
The memory of its waters
Knows where its heart must belong.

The years will have no meaning,
It will never take the blame,
Time will always be changeless,
The Mississippi the same.

The mighty Mississippi
Seems to be steadfast and true,
It will always be ageless,
And time will always be new.

CRUMBS OF COMFORT

The gentle touch of a child,
The comforting touch can prove
One little crumb of comfort
In anyplace that we move.

The gentle touch of a child,
Like the rivers that overflow,
Will stay on and forever
Its many blessings bestow.

The gentle touch of a child,
The memory will linger on,
Will always be there to comfort
When the people have older grown.

The gentle touch of a child,
Its gentleness to bestow,
Crumbs of comfort at sunset,
And rest brings the afterglow.

BEGIN AT HOME

When people start a mission—
Want to know where to begin?
The best place, begin at home,
Make a lovely world within.

The dear ones are all around,
Generations are the same,
When people think of themselves
Somebody else is to blame.

Deep within the human heart
Is always a lonely spot,
Someone always knows about,
That somebody else forgot.

When people start a mission—
Want to know where to begin?
Think of the dear ones at home,
All the dear ones try to win.

ALWAYS

Earth was covered with a cloud
When the voice of God spoke aloud.
The light of love was all around,
And earth became hallowed ground.

No longer darkness in the night,
Mercy and grace had brought the light,
The shining path to Heaven's throne
For souls who wish to follow on.

The Holy Spirit, Divine Love
Lifts the soul to Heaven above.
Where angels sing, God's children know,
The sunrise and the sunset glow.

Earth was covered with a cloud
When the voice of God spoke aloud,
Amid the world of noise and din,
The love of God always win.

COUNTRY DOCTOR

The good country doctor
Was a kind trusted friend,
When someone needed help,
His healing hand could mend.

The counsel of his words,
To be trusted and sure,
And many were the ills
His kindly words could cure.

When trouble came along,
He came without a call,
Comfort of his presence
Saved many from a fall.

The good country doctor,
Was a kind and trusted friend,
His presence brought the help
That only God can send.

MAN ON THE MOON

The man on the moon smiles on
The astronauts out in space,
He is waiting for them to land,
On his rugged smiling face,

The man on the moon is calm,
Cares not to compete with earth,
He sees the whole universe,
And cares not about its dearth.

There will always be a place,
Where calmness does not defy,
God's purpose in creation,
Or explain the reason why.

There will always be a place
For the moon and astronaut,
God alone knows the secret,
Of what the ages have taught.

ANSWERED

God in His way, somewhere, somehow,
In mercy has answered prayer,
In faith and love, we must believe.
Ready God's good gifts to receive.

Have faith to live, to look and find,
God has His way to remind,
A hungry need to believe,
Happy and thankful and not grieve.

This is a world bright and fair,
In the hands of God's loving care.
No one fails if they look and live,
Find strength in gifts God can give.

God in His way, somehow, somewhere,
In mercy has answered prayer,
The peace of mind that faith can see,
Is here for Eternity.

NEW WORLDS

Young people find new worlds
That they must conquer somehow,
They find most of the work done
Is by the sweat of the brow.

The world has regulations,
Old rules do not always fit,
There are many odd pieces
Must be placed bit by bit.

The people and places change,
Their thoughts do not always blend,
What was right yesterday
Today someone must build and mend.

Young people find new worlds
That they must conquer each day,
Today they build a new road,
That will be tomorrow's way.

ADVICE

Advice can be a good thing,
If it is the best advice;
Makes the world a better place,
It is something good to prize.

Advice to other people,
It is so much easier to give
Than to remember the good,
Try to practice it and live.

Advice is most always free,
Usually what some one thinks
While crossing over quicksand,
And seeing it before it sinks.

Advice can be a good thing,
Not something poor to discard,
It can be a gold jewel,
Or real silk sold by the yard.

VALENTINE

Lovers make a promise
On Saint Valentine's Day,
A Sweetheart's Paradise,
And hope it stays that way,

It takes a lovely dream,
A fragile flower sweet,
Two happy young lovers,
To make a world complete.

The happy little homes,
Family and fireside,
Where young lovers can dream,
The best in life provide.

Lovers make a promise
On Saint Valentine's Day,
Expect to be happy,
And happy days to stay.

SOLDIERS

Soldiers at home, soldiers abroad,
In their duty, carry a load;
They give time, service and they pray,
Honest efforts, working each day.

Loyal to family and homeland,
Patriots on duty to command,
Stars and Stripes they carry with pride,
They march together side by side.

Comrades left sometimes to sleep
In dark still waters, oceans deep,
Yet bravely they live, keeping on
Working, for their task must be done.

Soldiers at home, soldiers abroad,
All must travel a Service road,
They have no time to mourn and weep.
All soldiers have pledges to keep.

THE NEW RIVER GRAYS

We meet together, the New River Grays,
To reminisce over our yesterdays,
Not to commemorate their rise or fall,
But to honor our heroes, one and all.

Conditions around them molded their thought;
For the things they thought right, they nobly fought,
Their strength lives on in their children today,
Fighting for the ideals of the U.S.A.

Strength of character made them willing to die,
Hearts were broken when they severed a tie,
Loyalty that made them remember the clay,
Binds us together for the U.S.A.

Tenderly we look on the old, old flag,
But not for a moment does our allegiance lag,
Loyally we give all our strength today
TO OUR COUNTRY, OUR FLAG, OUR U.S.A.

VETERAN'S DAY

Veteran's Day is here again
With memories, heartbreak and pain.
Brave young soldiers who went away,
Loved ones at home to work and pray.

Veteran's Day is here again,
Roses fade in sunshine and rain,
Where the Stars and Stripes bravely wave,
Over a brave young soldier's grave.

Veteran's Day is here again,
Their records made without a stain,
Parents remember little boys
Who meant so much, their pride and joys.

Veteran's Day is here again
With memories, heartbreak and pain,
The brave young men who gave their best,
Where flowers are laid, soldiers rest.

PATRIOTISM

Patriotism means much more
Than waving a flag in the air,
It means loyalty, gratitude,
Honest service everywhere.

Patriotism means much more
Than the marching of feet on the street,
It means foundations tall and strong,
And never let wrong things defeat.

Patriotism lives forever,
It must be taught on bended knee,
The flag symbolizes love
When it is floating in the breeze,

Patriotism, a nation proud,
A people who stand tall and strong,
Loyalty to the land we love,
The lovely land where we belong.

WORLD APART

Poetry, music and art
Create a world apart,
Tenderness from the soul
Gives it a loving heart.

The lovely thoughts and sound
Will reach the world around,
The loving touch of hands,
From a heart that understands.

Lovely words line by line,
Gracious words that seem divine,
Like swelling tides that roll
From the depths of the soul.

Poetry, music and art
Create a world apart,
A holp place to start
From the depths of the heart.

SONS

Tall stalwart sons once were babies small,
Today's brave soldiers hear their country's call.
Loyally they hold their country's flag high
Beneath the stars at night, daytime's blue sky.

Tall stalwart sons once were babies small,
They know great truths of freedom must not fall,
They are lonely, not afraid, their love is true,
Each morning sun begins day anew.

Tall stalwart sons, once were babies small,
While God in Heaven sees them all,
Guardian angels must be there to see,
Minister to them wherever they may be.

Tall stalwart sons once were babies small,
Today's brave soldiers hear their country's call,
May God protect them while they are away,
Please God bring them home again we do pray.

WORTHY PEOPLE

Crowds of people on the street,
Close to church with empty pews,
They walk the street in darkness,
Never hear the Gospel News.

Crowds of people on the street,
There should be a deep concern,
A lost world is passing by
That knows not which way to turn.

Crowds of people on the street,
That someone should try to reach.
Somewhere there are hungry hearts,
Someone should be glad to teach.

Crowds of people on the street,
In every city and town,
That would like to hear the word,
Who is worthy of a crown.

GRANDFATHER'S FRUIT

Grandfather was a pioneer;
He cleared the land, left the fruit,
Carried the apple tree cuttings,
Grafted them to a crabapple root.

The coon grapevines climbed dogwood trees,
They were a lovely frosty black,
The purple and red fox grapes,
White fox grapes beside a fox track.

The fall grapes and muscadines,
Were tangy grapes after the frost,
They were the birds' best winter foods,
People never counted the cost.

Grandfather was a pioneer,
Let walnut and hickory trees stand,
Chestnut trees were in the fields,
He loved and cherished land.

MOTHER SAID

It is no disgrace to be poor,
To be dirty and lazy is.
God pity a poor lazy Tom,
God pity a poor lazy Liz.

It is no disgrace to be poor,
Honor can be a living Star,
The world admires honest people.
Some of their children will go far.

It is no disgrace to be poor,
For a hopeful spirit will pray,
Prayer and work go together,
And always finds a winning way.

It is no disgrace to be poor,
It cannot be counted as loss,
All people are just alike
Kneeling at the foot of the Cross.

GOOD PEOPLE

Good people grieve, but don't forget,
The people they have left behind,
They always look for the sunrise,
The gentle ties of love that bind.

Good people grieve but don't forget,
Their loyalty, kindness and love,
They live and move in peaceful ways,
Pray for direction from above.

Good people grieve but don't forget,
That other people have grief too,
They are kind and ready to help,
Through faith and prayer their strength renew.

Good people grieve but don't forget,
They are always looking ahead,
Live busy lives in honest work,
Honestly earn their Daily Bread.

BIRTHDAY

Happy Birthday to you, my dear,
Another day, another year,
Love and time will forever mix,
Another year, seventy-six,

Hope and dreams cannot run away,
For all of life has a birthday,
The golden sun that brightly beams,
Will bring to light its newer dreams,

To stay alive another year
And cherish well all it holds dear,
To carry light, a beacon strong,
The young will hear it sing a song.

A birthday wish, clever and sweet,
A happy day for all to greet,
The young may see so much to hold,
Rejoice and be glad, growing old.

MONDAY

Monday, the best day in the week
To organize the work we do,
After Sunday spent in Worship,
The week is easier to go through.

The many tasks that must be done,
That a working people must do,
The Holy Spirit will give help,
That will make the world always new.

The world is not so dull adn drab,
There is always a shining light,
The future world always a place
Where love can rise to higher height.

Monday, the best day in the week
To plan the days for work ahead,
Give honest work and honest time,
Each day to earn our daily bread.

TIMMY PATRICIA

Timmy Patricia,
Lovely lady is she,
Timmy Patricia,
A sweetheart she can be.

Timmy Patricia,
A loveworld welcomes you,
New Baby precious,
Happy Birthday to you.

Timmy Patricia,
We place you in God's care,
Where guardian angels
Always know you are there.

Timmy Patricia,
We pray for your Happiness,
May God's protecting care,
Guide you, protect and bless.

NO NEED

There is no need to guess
About what is to be,
Time will always reveal
The things that man should see.

Information will come,
Sometimes it is too late,
People have to accept
Whatever is their state.

To do the work at hand,
Will be the only way,
To be ready waiting,
Hope for a better day.

There is no need to guess
About what is to be,
Be ready and waiting,
For gifts time brings to thee.

SILVER WINGS

A pigeon has silver wings
That flash beneath the blue sky,
A lovely good morning world,
Silver flashes while they fly.

A pigeon has silver wings,
Signals of a busy life,
That flit across grain fields,
In humility and not strife.

A pigeon has silver wings
That gleam in fields of grain,
They are grateful to the farmer
For all the bountiful gains.

A pigeon has silver wings
That fly over barns and trees,
In gentle ways coo and talk,
About pleasant things like these.

LOVE THE LORD

Love the LORD thy God today,
For God has so loved thee,
He will guide you all through life,
For all of eternity.

Love the Lord thy God today,
Know that love can make you free,
All stormy paths will be clear,
God's guiding hand cares for thee.

Love the Lord thy God today,
In humility to pray,
Many cares in life will fade,
Burdens no longer dismay.

Love the Lord thy God today,
He will take away the grief,
Thy soul will grow much stronger,
Happy personal belief.

GOD'S HELPING HAND

Floods and famine, people die,
Tempests toss ocean waves,
Ages tell where people lie,
The hand of time cover graves.

Floods and famines, people dream,
Through all time and always will,
Searching for a sunshine beam,
Their empty hearts try to fill.

Floods and famines footprints left,
The paths that loved ones have made,
The earth cries out, hearts bereft,
Memories live, never fade.

Floods and famines, people die,
Searchers work because they care,
Love lives all time to defy,
God's helping hand, always there.

NOT HURRY

People should not hurry
When dealing with a soul,
BUT be careful and sure,
Of reaching the right goal.

A soul is too precious
To be in any haste,
Time is the greatest gift
No one should ever waste.

Life is a written page,
Made by the hand of time,
About the earthly things,
Or a future sublime.

People should not hurry
When dealing with a soul,
But cherish each moment,
Reach a heavenly goal.

QUEEN ANNE'S LACE

Queen Anne's Lace looks like snowflakes
In a field in summertime,
Fragile crowns that make them queen,
Storybook princess in a rhyme,

The butterflies pay homage
Close by the butterfly weed,
Brilliant blossoms glisten
While crops are going to seed.

Queen Anne's Lace looks like snowflakes,
Brings back dreams of wintertime,
The need for lovely summer
When flowers were in their prime.

The lovely fragile flowers,
Queen Anne's Lace is never plain,
Brings dreams of Queen and Prince,
To welcome them back again.

FAMILIES

Families should be good friends,
Beginning with mom and dad,
It will create hope and power,
Bring in good things, not bad.

Families should be good friends,
The world is always outside,
The ties of friendship and love,
Security can provide.

Families should be good friends,
Build a family stronghold,
Love is the road to heaven,
Worth more than power or gold.

Families should be good friends,
Beginning with mom and dad,
Families pray together
Learn to be happy and glad.

WALL

Anger can build a wall
That shuts a good world out,
Love that makes a good world,
Blessings could bring about.

Anger can build a wall
That is so very tall,
The darkness stays inside
Until the wall must fall.

Anger drives away hope
For love on sunny days,
It is always selfish,
And never stops to praise.

Anger can build a wall
That stands against all good,
Prayer is the answer,
Strength and spiritual food.

HIGHWAYS AND HEDGES

Highways and hedges can be,
On a crowded city street,
Lonely souls are always there
Where the lonely strangers meet.

Highways and hedges can be,
In any place people toil.
In the busy plants and mills,
Or people who till the soil.

Highways and hedges can be,
In the air or on the sea,
People need to know the Lord,
Hope and Salvation are free.

Highways and hedges can be,
Within the walls of a home,
God's love can reach anyplace
WHERE WANDERING CHILDREN ROAM.

FAITH

Stumbling block or stepping stone,
Which one of these shall it be?
The world always looking on,
Where someone will follow thee.

New troubles see the sunrise,
The just never forget,
God can drive away the clouds,
Send a glorious sunset.

In a world of affliction,
There is the sunshine and rain,
Same for the just and unjust,
Only faith can sing again.

Stumbling block or stepping-stone,
True faith is a steadfast friend,
Try to be a stepping-stone,
That God's healing love can send.

GOD'S GRACE

It is no easy road,
The straight and narrow path,
It is the only way
That souls escape God's wrath.

God made a set of rules,
Dictated by His love,
That lifts the soul of man
To higher heights above.

Above the sordid earth,
Where Esau's pottage grows,
Jacob accepted work,
The Will of God bestows.

It is no easy road,
The straight and narrow path,
God's Grace will clear the way,
And leave no aftermath.

TIME GIVES SOMETHING

Harder the blow, the less we feel,
Until all life becomes unreal,
Dreams of a lifetime all are gone,
Yet time is calling, says Go on.

Forgetting self, go find a place,
Endurance will come through God's grace,
Heaven is the same, God is there,
Mercy and help to always share.

No changes made, only we know,
Loss we found on the path of woe,
The little place we occupy,
The ages have seen live and die.

Harder the blow, the less we feel,
Yet time gives something that will heal,
After the grief, trouble and pain,
God's love will heal the heart again.

MISSING FACES

The hometown seems like strange places,
There are many missing faces,
Even the snowflakes that glisten,
Somehow seem to stop and listen.

It is time to stop and ponder
About the folks over yonder,
There seems to be sound of weeping,
Many loved ones are sleeping.

People left must service render,
To little ones young and tender
Give them love to take the places
Of the dear missing faces.

Tend a garden and be seeding,
For the children will be needing.
Love the children and render,
Be kind to them, loving tender.

FIRST SNOWFALL

The first snowfall on a new grave,
How cold and sad it is to see,
Fragile snowflakes like angel wings
Bring back sweet memories of thee.

The first snowfall on a new grave,
That comes in the silence of night,
The clean white blanket covers ground,
Gleaming jewels in the moonlight.

The first snowfall on a new grave,
Makes all the world look clean and white,
The grave is near yet seems so far,
No gentle voice to speak at night.

The first snowfall on a new grave,
Makes the world different to see,
The pure white snowflakes make Heaven near,
God in His way brings harmony.

PLANT

Plant a little flower,
Tend it so it will bloom,
And while it is growing
It drives away the gloom.

Plant a little flower,
Give it the loving care,
Make it happy to live,
It will grow anywhere.

Plant a little flower,
The years won't be as long,
While love is growing there,
It sings a happy song.

Plant a little flower,
Give it love and space,
Looking for tomorrow,
It will be there to grace.

TOMORROW

Thinking of tomorrow
Makes people brave today,
To give never borrow,
Is a far better way.

Thinking of tomorrow
With happy years ahead,
A world without sorrow,
With love and spiritual bread.

Thinking of tomorrow,
Many blessings bestow,
Today need not borrow,
Happy sunshine will show.

Thinking of tomorrow,
Heaven is there to share,
There will be no sorrow,
Blessings everywhere.

MOST PEOPLE

Most people are poets at heart,
In a dream world, thought, sight and sound,
Know a lovely world of beauty
That can change the world around.

Lovely thoughts bring Heaven closer,
There is glory in the sunset's glow,
All the sounds on earth are music,
So much harmony to bestow.

Common place things are beautiful
Apple blossoms and bees relate,
All of God's creatures on the earth,
Happy to watch and contemplate.

Most people are poets at heart,
All time is saying, it is true,
No one escapes earth and gladness,
The poet's world, including you.

THE GOD I KNOW

The God I know controls the universe,
His power in the sky, the seas, the lands,
Concerned enough to change the heart of man,
By His touch guides his feeble feet and hands.

His Word and the Holy Spirit live in me.
Wherever I am I know He will be,
His mercy knows my humble heart and heals,
Companionship with Him sets the soul free.

The God I know controls the universe,
In stormy seas the waves they toss and foam,
Trying to hide the troubled deep,
The restless waves they never feel at home.

The God I know controls the universe,
The soul of man is like the stormy deep,
All things in subjection under His feet.
Then to rest forever in peaceful sleep.

LET THE PEOPLE VOLUNTEER

Let the people volunteer,
To carry our country's flag,
Idealism will keep them,
Their loyalty never lag.

Let the people volunteer,
Then our country will be free,
The Stars and Stripes forever,
Were that all the world can see.

Let the people volunteer,
History will always state,
That service given through love,
Will make any country great.

Let the people volunteer,
Include both the young and old,
All ages cherish our Flag,
This our children have been told.

AS LONG

As long as someone worries
There will be no need to grieve,
There is someone left who cares,
And someone left to believe.

There will be a caretaker,
For all the treasures galore,
The lovely homes and mansions,
Many of them they will restore.

With all the lovely beauty
The present adds to the past,
To all the new tomorrows,
Will be anchored steadfast.

As long as someone worries,
Progress will be on the move,
The people who think and care,
They help the world to improve.

CALAMITY

Sometimes a calamity.
Will open another gate,
To see the tree of knowledge,
That will help to recreate.

Through all the days of sorrow,
The sun will begin to shine,
All through hours of darkness,
Is the Power Divine.

The helping hands will come forth
When the power of God is shown,
The world is a changed place,
Where the word of God is known.

Sometimes a calamity
Will open another gate,
Grace and the Holy Spirit
Lift the soul to higher state.

BARNYARD GOLF

Gardening is barnyard golf,
Many people often say,
The trophies are fruits to eat,
And the lovely flowers gay.

Gardening is barnyard golf,
Played with the hoe and spade,
Friendly hands to till the soil
Before summer seasons fade.

Gardening is barnyard golf,
To dream about when it snows,
All the lovely plans are made,
That in a dream garden grows and grows.

Gardening is barnyard golf,
That includes the birds and bees,
Lovely apple-blossom time,
Summer shadows under trees.

NEVER

Never give up a thing
When you are doing right,
Be steadfast and true,
Keep right on with the fight.

Some battles—only words
Some battles—only work,
With a code of ethics,
Honesty will not shirk.

The days may grow shorter,
The nights must longer be,
But time will soon provide
Enough daylight to see.

Never give up a thing
When you are doing right,
Any moment may bring
Victory to the sight.

FLOWERS WILL BLOOM

My dear sweet Vera Jane,
Here I am back again,
Another autumn day
With rolling clouds at play.

The autumn breeze is bold,
It is not very cold,
With the sky overcast,
The leaves are falling fast.

Since the rain the grass is green,
Forsythia blooms are seen,
Pretend a breath of spring
Is in their autumn fling.

Enough buds will be left,
Springtime won't be bereft,
Cheer is there and not gloom.
Springtime flowers will bloom.

LITTLE BIRDS

Little birds are flying by,
Going to their winter home,
They light in grainfields and eat,
Saying goodbye to the loam.

Little birds are flying by,
They seem to know where to stop,
They come back to the same place,
Where they found the last year's crop.

Little birds are flying by,
Always flying the same way,
Heaven built a road they know,
They never forget for a day.

Little birds are flying by,
They know where to eat and drink.
Their course is always so sure,
With never a missing link.

GOD SO LOVED

People are unhappy
And can never agree,
The things that they need most
And just what those things should be.

With trouble in the world,
With no line to divide,
Where can the peace be found
With all the world outside?

The world goes on and on,
Division cannot build,
Too soon voices must go,
No more cages to gild.

People are unhappy.
It was not meant to be,
God so loved the world
So it could better be.

IT IS GOOD

It is good to have memories
Of our loved ones who are gone.
It gives courage to work and pray
In this world, keep traveling on.

Memories of the trying years,
Sometimes there was a stormy day,
Then sunshine followed the clouds,
Then the blue skies came back to stay.

The stars would be there to twinkle,
Companions in the bright moonlight,
Families around the fireside,
Ready for another long night.

It is good to have memories,
Lovely memories that do belong,
Each generation learns to live,
Adds to the world another song.

THE WORLD

The world cannot enter Heaven,
All earthly things are left behind,
For Heaven is a perfect place
With eternal peace for the mind.

The world cannot enter Heaven,
Only souls that are upward bound,
Where truth and righteousness reign
The throne of mercy can be found.

The world cannot enter Heaven,
Where light and love always agree,
The transient wealth of Earth must fade,
Heaven's shining beauty to see.

The world cannot enter Heaven,
The ties on Earth always divide,
The healing balm of God's great love,
Welcomes pilgrims from the outside.

FRIENDS ARE FRIENDS

Friends are friends anywhere,
Day work or millionaire,
No difference to make
Love or friendly handshake.

Time changes many things,
Real friendship much joy brings
Money often forsakes,
Friends forgive the mistakes.

Love and a helping hand,
A friend will understand,
Pride often takes its toll,
It never heals a soul.

Friends are friends anywhere,
Day work or millionaire,
The touch of love is real,
Is always there to heal.

WORLDS

People in the same house
Are many worlds apart,
Some are in worlds of love,
Some worlds have no heart.

People in the same house
Know about worlds of hate,
See sadness and havoc,
That their worlds create.

People in the same house
Can never know the touch
That would make happiness,
That the worlds need so much.

People in the same house
Can extend friendly hands
That can blend together
A world that understands.

REMEMBER

Remember the high ideals
For which America stands,
Be strong-hearted when you vote.
That idealism demands.

Remember the great leaders,
By their sacrifices bought
The freedom for their children
Through tears they had often sought.

One nation, our U.S.A.
Under God our country dwells
The story through the ages
Its valiant history tells.

Remember high ideals
For which America stands,
Be proud of the great people.
The loyalty it commands.

RAINBOW GOLD

At the foot of the rainbow,
I have often been told,
If someone ever finds it,
There will be a pot of gold.

Chasing rainbows can be fun
When children are very small,
A rainbow in the cloud,
Children listen for its call.

Sometimes rainbows reach the earth,
Or it seems so far away,
But the ground gets very rough,
It leads children far astray.

At the foot of the rainbow,
Is a fortune seeker's dream,
Someone will go on seeking
As long as the rainbow beams.

WHY NOT ONE?

Seventeen children, not one,
Seventeen children all gone,
Seventeen children can't be,
Not one left to care for thee.

Wandering on land and sea,
Are they happy, are they free?
Hear the calls from the open roads,
With their burdens, heavy loads?

Are lands better far away,
Or have they been led astray?
Like the birds that migrate,
Do they find a better state?

Seventeen children by birth,
Wandering over the earth,
Why not one child just to keep,
Kiss goodnight and put to sleep?

STRANGER

Death is always a stranger,
With sadness the world must greet,
No way to escape the pain,
People bravely try to meet.

Death is always a stranger,
That will take a people home,
No way to get acquainted
With the stranger that will roam.

Death is always a stranger
That leaves the world so alone,
That it cannot heal the aches,
After it has come and gone,

Death is always a stranger,
No one ever understands,
But it will take the dearest,
To a far and distant land.

RED CARPET SERVICE

Red carpet service,
What do the words mean,
An offer of help,
Or service to gleam?

Red carpet service,
A good righteous move,
A kind gentle hand,
With goodness to prove.

Red carpet service,
Does it pave the way,
A way to begin,
And a way to stay?

Red carpet service,
What do the words mean,
The answer is there,
Go look at the scene.

STORYBOOK

Storybooks are good friends
That bring the world to you,
Tell about other lands,
The work that people do.

Books tell about children,
The games they like to play,
About how people live,
Things they like, words they say.

Books tell about ponies,
About the dogs and cats,
About the trees and birds,
Flowers that look like hats.

Books hold a friendly world
That can go anyplace,
Make the heart feel welcome,
And fill a friendly space.

HAPPIER

Children that walk to school
Are happier by far
Than children that ride a bus
Or the family car.

Children that walk to school
Can see the birds and trees,
See the apple blossoms,
And hear the humming bees.

Children that walk to school
Can talk with their good friends,
See swimming fish in pools,
Streams flowing around bends.

Children that walk to school
See many things that bless,
But most of all they know
What is real happiness.

COME HOME

Bread on the waters, please come home,
Bring back the crumbs that ride the foam,
Crumbs of comfort, blessed heart's ease,
Forever there, forever please.

Bread on the waters that cross seas
Are guided by a gentle breeze,
Crumbs of comfort that touch a hand
Send a thought to a distant land.

Bread on the waters, please come home,
Mission over no longer roam,
Crumbs of comfort that rides the waves
Love is the touch that gently saves.

Bread on the waters, time has past,
Crumbs of comfort forever last,
They cannot stay, forever roam,
Are best of all when they come home.

LOVE AND FIRESIDE

People like to travel,
And go from place to place,
Only folks that stay home
Can a home and fireside grace.

People like to travel,
Have no time to plant trees,
Tend a little garden,
The passerby to please.

People like to travel,
Have no time to make friends,
Or be a good neighbor,
For time and friendship blends.

People like to travel,
Their steps to retrace,
Long for fireside and home,
Where love and fireside grace.

WORTH MORE

Gentle voices, sweet smiles each day
Are worth more than gifts once a year,
Will bring much more happiness,
Create a world of love and cheer.

Gentle voices, sweet smiles each day,
Are worth more than silver and gold,
Than be kept for other day's wealth
No one knows it is there to hold.

Gentle voices, sweet smiles each day,
Are something wonderful to own,
Then no one will be cast away,
To be unhappy and alone.

Gentle voices, sweet smiles each day,
Are like angel wings that enfold,
A glimpse of Heaven can be seen,
Riches and wealth to never be sold.

WHERE?

Where are the friendly people,
All the little girls and boys,
That liked to hear church bells ring,
That brought the world many joys?

Where are the friendly people,
All the good neighbors and friends,
With their friendly helping hands,
That in all their friendship blends?

Where are the friendly people,
Who their friendly vigils keep,
Are they in some distant land,
Or have they all gone to sleep?

Where are the friendly people,
When will they come home to stay,
Be the lovely friends we know,
In the old-fashioned way?

SPRING

This is the first of March,
Green blades begin to peep.
The world is half awake,
The world is half asleep.

A warm and sunny day,
A gentle breeze can stir,
The world all looks to see
The pussy willow's fur.

The crocus buds are out,
And stay close to the ground,
The maple bloom is red,
Close by the songbird's sound.

This is the first of March,
A promise is in the air,
Springtime will soon be here,
Beauty everywhere.

MARCH

March has the reputation
Always being loud and shrill,
But it came in nice and warm,
And without a winter chill.

February brought the storms,
And devastated the towns,
March is bringing in the greens
And changing the winter browns.

The March wind may be roaring,
Not too far over the hill,
But the birds are all singing,
Not one little bird is still.

March has the reputation,
Always being loud and shrill.
Thank you for sunshine today,
You can be kind if you will.

AUTUMN

The oak and maple trees
Their autumn colors glow,
Mountainsides are lovely,
Their autumn colors show.

Birds have become restless,
The fields are golden brown,
The birds seek for shelter,
Sometimes they go to town.

The cattle search for grass,
Little partridges hide,
From all the ruthless guns,
Around the countryside.

The oak and maple trees,
In sympathy they see,
They can shelter the world,
Rejoice to live and be.

BETTY BAKER TRAIN

The Betty Baker Train
That came around the bend,
Whistles no longer blow,
The train came to an end.

The railroad track is gone,
Memory alone can tell,
Trucks now carry the freight
With no whistle or bell.

Signals for the crossing
Made children stop and look,
Now they learn about it
From a history book.

The Betty Baker Train
That came around the bend,
Vanished forever,
The story had to end.

JEWEL BOX

The world is a jewel box,
The sun shining on the sleet,
The evergreens make a dreamland,
But not for wandering feet.

Roads are covered with ice,
Icicles hang from the eaves,
The litle birds hide away
Under the evergreen leaves,

The cattle stay in the barn,
The children must go to school,
Only by self-discipline
Can the people keep a rule.

The world is a jewel box,
The sun shining on the sleet,
The world can wear the jewels
Have no feeling of defeat.

DO NOT BURDEN

Do not burden children,
Over today's sorrow,
They have their own problems
They must meet tomorrow.

Each generation knows
Troubles must not borrow,
Today's debts must be paid,
Not left for tomorrow,

The days are full of work,
Often there is trouble,
Any work left undone
Only makes it double.

Do not burden children
Over today's sorrow,
Teach the children ideals;
Help them meet tomorrow.

BRIGHT SIDE

Look at the bright side of life,
Through the stormy years ahead
Walk in faith through the darkness,
Pray for Spiritual Bread.

Look on the bright side of life,
Darkness will be all around,
May the flame of hope live on,
The crumbs of comfort be found.

Look on the bright side of life,
Other people look at you,
The candle that you carry
Will make a path strong and true.

Look on the bright side of life,
Other people have had fears,
Walk in faith through the darkness,
The light of hope dries the tears.

POUND CAKE

A pound cake is a man's cake,
My mother so often said,
Everybody eats it, likes it,
They are happy and well-fed.

One cup butter, two sugar,
Cream together, add four eggs,
One cup cream, three cups flour,
One teaspoon grated nutmeg,

Sift a teaspoon baking powder,
Sift several times with the flour,
Mix ingredients together,
Bake fifteen minutes and one hour.

Three hundred fifty degrees,
The right heat for it to bake,
Everybody eats it, likes it,
A pound cake is a man's cake.

CONGRATULATIONS

Dear Mr. and Mrs. Tommy,
We are glad that you have a son,
We do thank you for telling us
Of the birth of your little one.

May God bless you through the years,
Teach your little one, God is love.
Lead your little one to the church,
That joy comes from Heaven above.

There is much to be thankful for,
Rejoice, you have a little boy
May God's love direct you through life
And all your dreams and hopes employ.

All the world is a testing place
To find the source of purest gold.
May you find holy beauty
In the little hands that you hold.

THE RAIN FELL

The rain fell all night long,
And sang a nighttime song,
Autumn leaves were made clean,
Brightens the autumn scene.

The rain fell all night long,
A good-bye summer song,
Leaves were tinkling bells,
Falling the story tells.

The rain fell all night long,
That seemed so right and strong,
Colors gleam, autumn knows.
Hurries, blessings bestows.

The rain fell all night long,
And sand a nighttime song,
Morning world bright and gay,
Welcomes an autumn day.

FORGET

People forget to count
The good things that they see,
Only think of the things
They know should never be.

People forget to count
Humble violets that bloom,
That grow beside the path
To drive away the gloom.

People forget to count,
So many things they see,
The deeds done for others,
A better world to be.

People forget to count
The love a heart can hold,
The beauty of Heaven,
That a heart can enfold.

HALLOWEEN

Halloween was meant for children
To play and have a lot of fun,
Never to practice evil deeds,
Or hurt someone then to run.

Love the little children so much,
Then gently guide their little feet,
Teach them to be kind to others,
Unselfishly give them a treat.

Little children can be happy
When they are doing the most good,
They can practice the Golden Rule,
Be happy doing things they should.

Halloween was meant for children
To play and have a lot of fun,
They are like flowers and sunshine,
Their love will bless someone.

PEACE AND QUIET

When all is peace and quiet,
And there is nothing to fear,
There may be sudden destruction,
And disaster may be near,

When all is peace and quiet,
And faith has come in to stay,
The tomorrows may be sad,
But sufficient is today.

When all is peace and quiet,
Then faith will look up above,
People are not unhappy
When they depend on God's love.

When all is peace and quiet,
All the world may change its way,
Faith will always bring the peace,
The soul will not go astray.

DEPENDS

Someone depends on you,
No matter what you do,
Though they in darkness grope,
They will look to you in hope.

Someone depends on you
For a world that is new,
To try and lead the way,
A new world, a new day.

Someone depends on you,
This will always be true,
In darkness of night
They look for faith and light.

Someone depends on you,
A dependable clue,
To cross the mountaintops,
On wings that never stop.

RIGHTEOUS

A righteous man prayed to God,
Most humbly bowed to God's Will,
He humbly asked for direction,
Bravely climbed another hill.

A righteous man prayed to God
For strength to be faithful always,
That he might do the will of God,
To give God the glory and praise.

A righteous man prayed to God
For lonely people who are afraid,
His prayer for others made him strong,
God gave him strength to give them aid.

A righteous man prayed to God,
Heaven and earth were always new,
He made a pathway to Heaven
Others can see while passing through.

CLEAR MAP

Make a clear map to show
Wheer the people should go,
Make a clear path to see,
Clear of useless debris.

Make a clear map to show,
People will better know,
Work to do, words to say,
To make a better way.

Make a clear map to show
Where blessings can bestow,
Ease to a weary heart
That will never depart.

Make a clear map to show
How that goodness can grow,
Let not others deride,
Or turn the good aside.

GIFTS

I give to you a rose,
Its fragrance there to seek;
I give you a poem,
Words to forever speak.

Rhythmic beauty of words,
Both poetry and prose,
Can be symbolized
By fragrance of the rose.

Little stars that twinkle
Have voices of their own,
They all need companions,
So they won't be alone.

I give you a poem,
A lovely world to own,
With sunrise and sunsets,
Never leaves you alone.

WEARY

Old people do grow weary,
Their feet are tired and slow,
Trailing on behind a crowd,
They have nowhere they can go.

Old people do grow weary,
They look around in dismay,
Forgotten are the answers
That they knew on yesterday.

Old people do grow weary,
While they should patiently wait,
They still have all the tomorrows
To live in another state.

Old people do grow weary,
They create a mournful sound,
They should try to keep singing,
And know they are upward bound.

CHRISTIANS

Christians have many troubles,
With ashes, graves and pitfalls,
Jesus is there to help them,
His Mercy hears all their calls.

Christians have many troubles,
A helper is standing by,
The little lambs call to Him,
He can hear their lonely cry.

Christians have many troubles,
It will always be the same,
A separated people
That will glorify His name.

Christians have many troubles,
With ashes, graves and pitfalls,
There will always be comfort,
His mercy hears all their calls.

TREASURE

Memory is a treasure chest,
The gentle people we have known,
Who lived noble lives and left,
Precious memories older grown.

The mothers sang sweet lullabys.
The songs that could never grow old,
While fathers gave to their country,
The loyalty worth more than gold.

The people that lived then were poor,
But the women were ladies fair,
The men were noble gentlemen,
They were patriots anywhere.

Memory is a treasure chest,
Precious memories older grown,
Time will increase their value,
The riches wonderful to own.

LIGHTS

Lights must be kept burning
When driving in a fog,
To make a safer world,
When driving in the smog.

Lights must be kept burning
So that people can see,
And safely travel on
To the place they must be.

Lights must be kept burning,
The lights will be a guide,
In a safe good journey,
No one will turn aside.

Lights must be kept burning
When driving in a fog,
The journey will be safe,
Never end in a bog.

BUSY PEOPLE

Busy people need the Lord,
That work always be well done.
They could reach lost people,
Many people could be won.

With a dedicated life
Spent in service and love,
The world looks on with respect,
The way they work, where they move.

Busy people need the Lord,
They have so much they can give,
Their honest labor will show
The world the way that they live.

Busy people need the Lord,
Each moment they need Him more,
God's blessings are always there
And are greater than before.

PROBLEMS

There will always be problems—
Problems old, problems new.
There will be mountains to climb,
Trying for a better view.

There will be rivers to cross,
Where roads are rocky and rough,
Some answers cannot be found,
That will be answers enough.

Little things seem like mountains,
The bigger things seem quite small,
A steady hand for a guide,
Will prevent heartbreak and fall.

There will always be problems—
Problems old, problems new.
And problems won't amount to much
When people know what to do.

BETTER

Better stop in the beginning,
When a thing is known to be wrong,
Than to live in a world apart,
Where there is no place to belong.

Better stop in the beginning
Than try to go on—be a part—
For people are not happy
Trying to live without a heart.

Better stop in the beginning,
And think before making a leap,
Than live in a world of darkness,
And have nothing lovely to keep.

Better stop in the beginning,
And pray to find a better way.
All the world will rejoice with you
That you travel by light of day.

FELLOWSHIP

In fellowship with the saints,
Opportunity to do good,
The Holy Spirit moves on
To mark where the martyrs stood.

In fellowship with the saints,
Blessed be the tie of love,
Lifts the soul from sordid earth,
Closer to Heaven above.

In fellowship with the saints,
Worship makes a Holy Ground,
The soul can reach higher heights,
When God's Holy Ways are found.

In fellowship with the saints,
Across the many long years,
Eases pain of weary hearts
And will wipe away the tears.

KEEP

Keep the lights burning bright,
Bring forth steadfast light,
People can see and know,
The safest way they should go.

Keep the lights burning bright,
To show which roads are right,
So there will be no dismay,
Starless night or foggy day

Keep the lights burning bright,
And keep the goal in sight.
Know the things right and true,
Nobler paths to pursue.

Keep the lights burning bright,
There will be faith, not fright,
Make a path straight and true
For folks who follow you.

BLESSING

God is always blessing thee.
Through you He can bless others,
Through His mercy and Grace see
All men are needy brothers.

God is always blessing thee,
Through all the joys and sorrows
God's Grace suffcient will be
The future, God's tomorrows.

God is always blessing thee,
In Him we have our being,
The truth makes His children free,
Heavenly truths they are seeing.

God is always blessing thee,
Love will keep His children moving,
The touch of mercy will be,
While God's love they are proving.

DO NOT TOUCH

Do not touch forbidden fruit,
Or walk a forbidden path,
Unhappy souls soon will find
The touch of God's Holy Wrath.

Do not touch forbidden fruit,
Or let the heart go astray,
Far better roads can be sought
That will lead a fairer way.

Do not touch forbidden fruit,
Take time to live, love and pray.
There is waiting tomorrow,
Good things that make a glad day.

Do not touch forbidden fruit,
God's love is ready to prove,
His love will make the way clear
To show the right way to move.

MAKE THEM WELCOME

Invite one hundred people
Highways and hedges to search,
Go tell them that you love them,
Invite them to come to church.

Be sure to make them welcome
In a fellowship of love,
Leave all earthly things behind,
See Heavenly worlds above.

The people will surely know
That there is a Golden Rule.
Read the Bible together;
It is time for Sunday School.

Invite one hundred people,
Surely somebody will come,
The world is full of people,
Longing for a good church home.

WHO?

Who will answer the call
When the good shepherds search?
Who will ease a heartache,
And bring someone to church?

Who will teach the Bible
That people have not heard,
Worship the Lord thy God,
And teach His Holy Word?

Who will care for the weak,
Supply their many needs,
A ministry of love,
Doing Christian deeds?

Who will answer the call
To the Good Shepherd's knock?
People with open hearts,
With love their hearts unlock.

ROMANCE

Romance will never die
As long as people dream,
And look for the sunshine
In each bright golden beam.

Romance will never die
As long as people love,
Listen for flittings
An innocent dove.

Romance will never die
Because of an old age,
Each day in human life
Will add another page.

Romance will never die,
But will cherish and give
Unselfish love to life
To eternally live.

NO DIFFERENCE

People see no difference
In views when growing old,
The view is as lovely,
And sunsets are of purest gold.

Heaven is a glorious place
Where the streets of finest gold,
And no one ever cares at all
Or worries about growing old.

A dream is always in view,
Where there is no place for regret.
And all of life is good to know,
To remember and not forget.

Old people see no difference,
They retain the faith of a child,
Know that heaven will be their home,
Their world will be gentle and mild.

BUILDERS

Little boys are engineers,
They can build their castles fair,
Little girls will live in them,
Granny in her rocking chair.

Mother and father live there,
Grandfather with desk and books,
A world full of lovely dreams,
That know how a princess looks.

Fireside and love in the home,
A place for a fairy queen,
Builders find a world complete
Where they can their treasures glean.

Little boys are engineers,
They can build their castles fair,
They can take inventory,
All good blessings declare.

71

COVERED BRIDGE

The man who built the Covered Bridge
Used locust beams big and strong,
With honest pride he built the Bridge.
To the future it would belong.

The Covered Bridge was shelter
For people in time of storm,
Children, horses and the wagons,
They could be protected and warm.

The clear River beneath the Bridge
Was often a baptismal pool,
Close by was the little white church
That taught people the Golden Rule.

A concrete bridge was built down the stream,
The wooden bridge was thrown away,
Pictures of the Wooden Bridge
Bring tears to the children today.

The Covered Bridge was a landmark,
In history books brings back the dreams,
The little children dream again,
With tears they see the sparkling streams.

DREAM ON

Dream on, sweet young dreamers,
Be glad you are twenty,
The world a lovely place,
Romance is aplenty.

The first forty is nice,
Lovely world of people,
Memories are precious,
Weddings and church steeple.

Forty years repeated,
Makes a problem weighty,
There is so much wonder,
About second eighty.

It will be just the same,
A new life beginning,
Live the first eighty well,
Heaven will be winning.

Dream on, sweet young dreamers,
Time is always calling,
The future is with God,
No one will be falling.

MOMENTS OF TIME

When today becomes yesterday
And tomorrow becomes today,
The importance of time is shown
In the work we do and words we say.

Yesterday is the foundation
To all the things we have today,
Today should build for tomorrow,
So the world will not go astray.

Moments of time are important,
Misspent time make troubles mount,
When time is spent in doing good,
Brings worthwhile things that really count.

When today becomes yesterday
And tomorrow becomes today
May roads we pave be strong and right,
Time for living, to work and pray.

BEAUTIFUL THOUGHTS

Thinking beautiful thoughts
And doing it each day,
Doing beautiful deeds,
Never running away.

Through all the winter storms,
Through all the summer heat,
To try and keep working
With never a retreat.

Time has a way of telling,
The good things that will last,
There would be no future
Without some kind of past,

Thinking beautiful thoughts
Will much better create
A state of mind so strong
The soul will elevate.

74

COMFORT

When grief is overwhelming
And trouble is at the door
The helping hand of God's love
Will be needed more and more.

When grief is overwhelming
And trouble is at the door,
The helping hand of God's love
Can our peace of mind restore.

When grief is overwhelming
And trouble is at the door
God can give the peace of mind
That is greater than before.

When grief is overwhelming
And trouble is at the door
The Holy Spirit comforts
And will be there over and over.

BLUEBIRDS

Bluebirds are for happiness,
Nesting in the cherry tree,
Children love and watch them,
They are so happy and free.

Apple blossom petals fall
When the little bluebirds fly,
Children watch their flitting wings,
Silhouetted against the sky.

Little birds eat the cherries,
Little children are so glad
They most gladly share the fruit,
The little birds are not bad.

Bluebirds are for happiness,
They make springtime bright and gay,
The world is a better place
When the bluebirds come to stay.

SMILES

Smiles can say many things,
More than words can express,
Smiles tell of grief and joy,
A world of happiness.

Smiles say many things,
Memories of the past,
Of hopes for tomorrow,
As long as time shall last.

Smiles can say many things,
Stories today can tell,
Where people live and love,
A land where angels dwell.

Smiles can say many things
Of all the dreams come true,
A land where lovers live,
Of worlds both old and new.

PARKING LOT

They made a parking lot
Where the old building stood,
Only memory tells
About the brick and wood.

The name across the front,
Business was done there,
Friendly faces of friends
That came around the square.

Happy years were spent there
But people soon forgot,
Today the pavement square
Another parking lot.

A few will remember
With heartache and regret,
Look forward to a place
Where no one will forget.

TRANSIENT

A man came to the door
With a gift in his hand,
He was asking for work
And making no demand.

Hunger was in his eyes,
A lost despairing look,
Many days without food
That made a storybook.

He did a little work,
Then the man felt free,
As the gift he had brought,
The honey from the bee.

For a moment or a day,
Humble and alone,
The poor man found help.
Now he can journey on.

CUSTODIANS

Some people are custodians
And always think of others,
Never let anyone starve,
Think that all men are brothers.

Some people are custodians,
While gardens they are tending
They are always doing good,
Find something to be mending.

Some people are custodians,
Careful in work they are doing,
They always live honest lives,
While work they are pursuing,

Some people are custodians,
So gentle in their living,
They do not mind humble tasks,
They rejoice to be giving.

TRAIN WHISTLE

Hear that lonesome train whistle,
Its coming around the bend,
It's coming around the bend,
Hear that lonesome train whistle,
As if all the world must end.

Hear that lonesome train whistle,
The whistle has much to say,
Hear that lonesome train whistle,
Someone calling out today,

Hear that lonesome train whistle,
Someone is calling a friend,
Hear that lonesome train whistle,
There are many things to mend,

Hear that lonesome train whistle,
Train coming around the bend,
Hear that lonesome train whistle,
A messenger it must send.

ACCEPTED TIME

Today is the accepted time
To remember the Lord thy God,
To see humility and love,
As the greatest chastening rod.

Today is the accepted time
To forget self, most humbly bow,
Heaven's Kingdom is now at hand,
A surrendered life must be now.

Today is the accepted time
The tomorrows may be too late,
Rise today above the shadows,
Walk steadfastly through Hea'en's Gate.

Today is the accepted time,
God will pardon those who heard,
Those who listen and love today,
And accept God's most Holy Word.

TURN PAGES OF HISTORY

Turn the pages of history,
Look at ideals of the past,
Then look at all the world today
To see the ideals that will last.

Turn the pages of history,
Look at the best foundation stone,
The era when buildings were made,
See the strongest that stand alone.

Turn the pages of history,
It can show the world today's truth,
So fewer mistakes will be made,
It will be there to aid the youth.

Turn back the pages of history,
Search for all the noble and true,
It is worthwhile to see the light,
Count the stars in skies of blue.

LONELY PEOPLE

Lonely people, lonely town,
Milling crowds are all around,
Looking, trying to see
Where friendly faces are found.

Lonely people on the street
Waiting for someone to speak.
Lonely people do not know
Where to find comfort they seek.

Lonely people, lonely town,
Turn away from paths they know,
Looking up, looking down,
Never knowing where to go.

Lonely people, lonely town,
Seeking love and friendly hands,
There must be friends somewhere to find,
A new world in happy lands.

LITTLE WORLD

There is a little world,
A little world apart.
That is a special place
That lives within the heart.

It is a world of love
So comforting to know,
Love reaches out to touch,
Its blessings to bestow.

The time is passing fast,
So many things to do,
The world will always change,
The road is always new.

There is a little world,
That never has a rift,
Love can keep it going,
To bless and to uplift.

EVALUATE

People learn to evaluate,
On the road of life growing old,
They learn to cast aside the dross,
To treasure love much more than gold.

People learn to evaluate
The music in a lovely song,
They learn it can tell a soul
Heavenly places to belong.

People learn to evaluate
The beauty of a singing bird,
So close to Heaven while on earth
They are sure God has heard each word.

People learn to evaluate
Each day that passes casts its mold,
Thus life will have its full measure,
Treasures that are worth more than gold.

SOMEWHERE

There is a dreamland somewhere,
A land where dreams come true,
Where fairies dream all night long,
Beneath starry skies of blue.

Little fairies are happy,
Secure in the arms of love,
They know someone cares for them.
Where fairy ships sail above.

The pastures soft and green,
Shepherds watch over the flock,
Where the little lambs at play,
Listen for the Shepherd's knock.

There is a dreamland somewhere,
A land where dreams come true,
Shepherds and lambs rest at night,
Happy to begin each day new.

HAPPY BIRTHDAY

Happy Birthday, Lucy Lyndall
May God bless you, dear little girl.
Jewel to love, a lovely pearl
That brings so much joy to the world.

May health and happiness be yours.
All of life be beautiful for you,
May you find the happy sunshine,
Your days be like diamonds of dew.

May peace and love be yours always,
The sunrise bring your heart a glow,
Sweet dreams be yours in the sunset,
With many pleasant years to know.

May birthdays always be happy,
So many things we wish for you,
May Heaven and Earth be kind to you,
The stars be bright, the skies be blue.

DAUGHTERS OF THE CONFEDERACY

Daughters of the Confederacy—
The reason it came to be,
Historical, education,
Memorials the world can see.

The wives, widows and mothers,
The daughters and sisters knew
The need for benevolence.
Their service together grew

The Confederate soldiers gave
Until they had given all,
A proud and historic past,
With its patriotic call.

History and truth keep its records,
The Jefferson Davis Highway
With its markers from the U.D.C.
Honors a great statesman today.

Monuments and memorials,
For all human needs they care,
For schools, homes and hospitals,
The U.D.C. will be there.

THE CROSS

The Cross is not a thorn in the flesh
Nor is it made of life's cares and pain,
It is concern for all lost people
Who need Christ and to be born again.

To be born in the newness of life,
To open one's heart to the cry for love,
To see the new heaven and earth
Living in the people who move.

The Cross is not a thorn in the flesh
But living above the strife and greed,
Always holding out a helping hand,
A living witness in time of need.

To live and witness a world apart,
A world of beauty for us to see,
A world in which we can always be,
A life to live for all eternity.

The cross is not a thorn in the flesh
Nor is it made of life's cares and pain,
But waiting for all newness of life,
Rejoicing for the souls born again.

BIRTHDAY

Any day is a birthday,
There is always something new,
To challenge the very best
Work that a person can do.

Any day is a birthday,
As a new day will always be,
Tomorrow is a promise
That folks will happier be.

Any day is a birthday
That will last throughout the new year,
Faith makes the heart grow stronger,
There will be nothing to fear.

Any day is a birthday,
All the little children know,
Old people must not lose faith,
All people must older grow.

WORDS

Tender words of mercy
Are never out of place,
Always need for kindness,
A special world of grace,

God is always giving,
His people need to see,
Be happy in their souls,
For all humanity.

Earth is a stopping place
For God's children to see
To learn about the Lord,
Love and mercy are free.

Tender words of mercy
Will never fade away,
Will live on forever,
In God's Eternal Day.

CORN TASSELS

Corn tassels in the field,
A lovely russet brown,
Jewels in the autumn
That make a lovely crown.

Cattle across the fence
Have hungry wistful eyes,
Corn is something to eat
And something that they prize.

Hungry instinct tells them
The crops across the fence
Will give to them the life
That they accutely sense.

Corn tassels in the field
Will supply their winter's needs,
The cattle must be fed,
There must be food and seed.

BIRDS

The birds were all talking,
Were noisy and gay,
In a farewell party,
Frost was not far away.

They told about winter,
In a sweet farewell song,
They go to a winter home,
Where all the birds belong.

They twitter and they chirp.
Next spring will call them back,
To all the same places,
They never lose a track.

They are faithful to mates,
Remember all their friends,
Always in good standing,
Live where the season sends.

WILL COME A SHEPHERD

A church without a pastor,
With no shepherd in the flock,
No one to answer the door
When little lambs come to knock.

A church without a pastor
Needs to be a praying place.
When the church comes together
The Holy Spirit will grace.

A church without a pastor
In fellowship it must be,
The Holy Spirit directs
A righteous way to see.

A church without a pastor
Must turn to God in its need,
Pray that a shepherd will come
To all the little lambs feed.

LITTLE FLOCK

It is your Father's good pleasure
To give you the best little flock,
Await at the door and listen,
Soon you will hear Your Father's knock.

He gives to you the kingdom,
Listen well for the Master's call,
Living in the hollow of his hand,
He sees the sparrows fall.

He cares for little lambs,
Provides for them grass in fields,
He plants for them seeds of love,
Controls the earth and harvest yields.

Trust ye the Lord all ye children,
The doors of the kingdom unlock,
It is your Father's good pleasure
To give you the best little flock.

WE THANK YOU

We thank you, Mr. President
For doing the best that you can
To bring about lasting peace
According to God's Divine Plan.

We thank you, Mr. President,
Seeking things that are just and right,
For seeking God's Divine Guidance,
God's holy power, His great might.

We thank you, Mr. President,
For speaking to hearts of our youth,
May young people know the good things,
Know the ideals of justice and truth.

We thank you, Mr. President,
For thinking of both youth and age,
We pray God will give you wisdom,
The Book of Life to read page by page.

WE PRAY

We pray for our soldier boys,
Who are prisoners of war,
We pray that peace will come,
That God will remove each bar.

We pray for our soldier boys,
Who languish in distant lands,
We pray for mercy and Peace,
The Ministry of God's hands.

We pray for our soldier boys,
For their families and friends,
May they find the comfort they need,
When the sad cruel war ends.

We pray for our soldier boys,
May there be lasting peace,
May God's blessing rest on them,
Their happiness never cease.

KEEP WORKING

Keep working hard today,
Planning for tomorrow,
The way to ease a pain,
And heal today's sorrow.

Keep working hard today,
No time for forgetting,
Be too busy for grief,
Lose no time regretting.

There will be stormy days,
Days of stormy weather,
Hold out a helping hand,
Work along together.

Keep working hard today,
Giving, never borrow,
The cup of love lives on,
Overflows tomorrow.

FRIENDLY HANDS

Hold out friendly hands today
To someone who is in need,
So many hungry people
Appreciate a kindly deed,

Hold out a friendly hand today,
Tomorrow may be too late,
To try and save some poor soul
From a brokenhearted fate.

Hold out a friendly hand today
And give to the world the best,
Some poor tired weary soul
May need to find peace and rest.

Hold out a friendly hand today
To erase the thing that mars,
There is a silver lining
That is found beyond the stars.

COURAGE

Courage expects happiness
With all the lovely things it brings;
Courage expects happiness
With the lovely songs it sings.

Courage expects happiness
With today's time to employ,
Courage expects happiness
With tomorrow to enjoy.

Courage expects happiness
While weary climbing a hill,
Courage expects happiness
It knows courage can fulfill.

Courage expects happiness
And to all its dreams it clings,
Courage expects happiness,
It is an angel on wings.

I WILL GO

I will go to Sunday school
Though it may be lonely there,
To teach myself a lesson,
To read the Word and prepare.

I will go to Sunday School,
I will meditate and pray,
To be faithful through the week,
Tomorrow another day.

I will go to Sunday School,
I may be the only one there,
I will thank God for Sunday
And know that the day is fair.

I will go to Sunday School
In our dear friendly home church,
The Holy Spirit is there,
I no longer have to search.

OPTIMISM

Why should people wait so long
To write a New Year's letter.
Why not write someone each day?
That would be so much better.

Scatter a little more cheer
Where a little sunshine is beaming.
A few more lights will be there,
A world can see them gleaming.

Happiness can always be found
When kindness is the keeper,
Someone will look for the light,
No more the lazy sleeper.

Why should people wait so long
To make the world more cheery,
So write another letter.
Forgetting to be dreary.

THE PILGRIM

The pilgrim in the valley
Often grows tired and sleeps,
But Jesus in His mercy
Saves, holds fast always keeps.

The Pilgrim in the valley,
Often weary and alone,
When he sees the Savior
Has closer to heaven grown.

The pilgrim in the valley
Accepts God's mercy and grace,
No place is ever too dark
To find Peace and resting place.

The pilgrim in the valley,
Is in every walk of life,
The Holy Spirit will keep,
Free weary souls from all strife.

FOOTPRINTS

Footprints in the fields
no longer to be seen,
The path no longer there,
The grass is growing green.

Footprints in the fields
Have all faded and gone,
The robins stop awhile,
Then they, too, pass on.

Footprints in the fields,
Cattle in wonder gaze,
Search the landscape awhile,
Then cross the fields to graze,

Footprints in the fields,
Friendly memories grow,
Keep footprints in the fields
Where they were long ago.

HONOR THE COLLEGE

Honor the college campus,
With dignity and respect,
As a great place of learning
That is worthy to protect.

Honor the college campus,
Wisdom and virtue are taught,
Where future generations
Found the knowledge that it sought.

Honor the college campus
That has made a nation great,
Where youth went for training,
Created a noble state.

Honor the college campus
With dignity and respect,
Give thanks to God, for the work,
People that serve and direct.

NEW YEAR'S DAY

Give thanks for New Year's Day,
Thanking God for the past,
The blessings of last year,
The memories that last.

Thanksgiving for the gifts,
And blessings through the year,
Brings hope for tomorrow,
And fills the soul with cheer.

The earth in its beauty
Speaks in a special way
To supply human needs
For those who work and pray.

Give thanks for New Year's Day,
Go forward without fear,
Faith in a helping hand,
God's love is always near.

SHOULD NOT GRIEVE

Old people should not grieve
About things they have to leave,
Old are the blessings of wealth,
That accumulates from health.

Old people should not grieve,
They learn to live and believe,
They have seen time right a wrong,
While life and love sings a song.

Old people should not grieve,
Time has no way to deceive,
Age and wisdom bring to light
Truth is seen in all its might.

Old people should not grieve,
Think of time as a loom to weave
A mantle to wear, love and grace,
Home at last a resting place.

SNOW

The snow is deep and white,
The moon is shining bright,
Like a fairyland dream,
For each lovely moonbeam.

Tree shadows in moonlight,
Look different at night,
The fences, barns and sheds,
Protect the sleepy heads.

Fields look like distant lands,
Without daytime demands,
The little birdlings cheep,
Then gently go to sleep.

The snow is deep and white,
The moon is shining bright,
Protecting field and sod,
Seem very close to God.

SING A SONG IN THE NIGHT

Christians sing with tears in their eyes,
A song in the heart through darkest night,
Heaven near a glorious prize,
The glory of eternal light.

Christians sing with tears in their eyes,
A song of peace, a song of right,
Eternal hope never denies,
The glorious view that is in sight.

Christians sing with tears in their eyes,
Guardian angels are always near,
To heal all troubles that arise,
The light of hope drives away fear.

Christians sing with tears in their eyes,
A song in the heart through darkest night,
Something to love never despise
The glory of eternal light.

HATE

Hate is a consuming thing,
Will all its burdens bring,
To fill the world with dismay,
Lead little lambs far astray.

Hate is a consuming thing,
It cannot a blessing bring,
Its work can only destroy
All the hands in its employ.

Hate is a consuming thing,
Will always wound with its sting,
Hate creates a world unreal,
Has no mercy, cannot heal.

Hate is a consuming thing,
Has no joyous way to sing,
Only love can destroy gloom,
Where love lives hate has no room.

THE FRIENDLY CHURCH

The friendly church with friendly chimes,
The call of welcome at all times,
Little children won't you please come
And make this church your home?

Sunday morning and Sunday School,
The Word of God, the golden rule,
The friendly chimes are calling. Come,
We welcome you, please do not roam.

Worship service, reverence taught,
Friendship and fellowship are sought,
That lives forever in the heart,
Eternal things never depart.

The friendly church with friendly chimes,
Its call of welcome at all times,
Doors are open, a place to pray
We welcome you, please come today.

NEVER BE AFRAID

Never be afraid
To be left alone,
God keeps His children,
Takes care of His own.

Faith and love holds fast,
Through days of distress,
Heartbreak may be there,
So will happiness.

The world will go on,
There will always be
God's protecting love
For eternity.

Never be afraid
To be left alone,
Faith in God will keep
Children older grown.

SNOWBOUND BIRDS

The sun has just come out,
Jewels are in the snow,
For every sunbeam
There is a lovely glow.

Ice is on the highway,
For birds a skating rink.
Hungry little creatures,
Without water to drink.

There is no food on ice,
The birds are there to say,
Who will scatter some crumbs
To feed the bords today.

The sun has just come out,
Jewels are in the snow,
The little birds are begging
For food before they go.

CATTLE

The cattle look lonely
When walking in the snow,
They only follow paths
Where they are told to go.

They search for the feed trough,
The scattered bits of hay,
They like green grass better,
Prefer it any day.

They try to find shelter,
To stay away from harm,
When snow is in the wind
It is hard to keep warm

The cattle look lonely,
With earnest begging eyes,
The sun has just come out,
What a happy surprise!

THE NEW YEAR

The New Year is on its way
Eight winter days have gone by,
To promise a lovely year,
To people who work and try.

The New Year will bring its changes,
With so many things to learn,
Experience is always new,
Cause a great deal of concern.

It is best to feel concern.
People will more able be,
To know, feel love for others,
A broader vision to see.

The New Year is on its way,
The years can most gracious be.
Each day a glad good morning,
For blessed Eternity.

PEOPLE WHO WORK

People must not stop to grieve
Over their possessions lost,
For each moment of heartbreak
Will always add to the cost.

All time lost in grieving
Would help a future to build,
Someone could make a garden
That loving hands have tilled.

There is always a new road
That the moon and stars can see,
A new work ready to begin,
Where hearts again can be free.

People must not stop to grieve,
All the world is crying out,
People who work find the answer,
What the world is all about.

SAYING

Saying Happy New Year
For one day in each year
Is not enough to last
Or bring enough of cheer.

One day, Happy New Year,
When days and weeks go by.
Memory of New Year
Can only bring a sigh.

Happy New Year is past,
Each day is something new,
Each day something special
With something good to do.

Saying Happy New Year
Can last all the year through,
Show new ways to travel
Where roads are always new.

TRY

Try to think cheerful thoughts
And drive away the gloom,
There is always a need,
There is plenty of room.

Troubles will always be,
And keep on coming in,
Never gets discouraged,
It always hopes to win.

To be an optimist
Is a much better way,
It makes a happy life,
Brings good thoughts for the day.

Try to think cheerful thoughts,
Always a room and place,
To drive away a frown
And have a smiling face.

WIND

The clouds are rolling high,
The wind is coming in,
The little kittens listen,
Know that the wind will win.

The cattle seek shelter
From wind behind the hill,
Soon the trees will bend,
The wind sounds loud and shrill.

Little birds are quiet,
Not a chirp can be heard.
Silence tells the story
From animals and bird.

The clouds are rolling high.
The wind is coming in,
It tells the same story
Where all the winds have been.

TOMORROW

The time will never end,
People have often said,
Time goes on forever,
Tomorrow is ahead,

Today's preparation,
To work a little while,
Tomorrow always there,
So meet it with a smile.

People need not complain
About burdens today,
Tomorrow is nearer
Than anyone can say.

The time will never end,
Tomorrow always new,
And no one counts the time,
The work it has to do.

GOD'S WONDERLAND

The New Jerusalem
Is God's great Wonderland,
The Holy Spirit reigns
In souls that understand.

A New Heaven and Earth
Is set apart by love,
Holy City of God,
Part of Heaven above,

The world is looking on,
At God's great wonderland,
Know God is on His Throne,
His kingdom to command.

The New Jerusalem
Is God's great wonderland,
The humble know His touch
And love His guiding hand.

IDEALS

Mix ideals with ambition.
Then look at the stars at night,
The sun above mountaintops
That is somewhere shining bright.

Mix ideals with ambition,
All creation glorify,
The earth will all be blessed,
The ages will not deny.

Mix ideals with ambition
When doing the smallest things,
Harmony of right and justice,
A lovely harmony sings.

Mix ideals with ambition,
All the world will better be,
Each day will gradually build,
For peace in eternity.

GOLD MINES AT HOME

The dissatisfied people,
The answers they do not know,
They can find no place to stay
And do not know where they can go.

The dissatisfied people
Break the friendly ties that link,
Because they travel too fast
And never take time to think.

The dissatisfied people
Often have gold mines at home,
At the foot of the rainbow,
And would never need to roam.

The same stars shine in the night,
The same sun lights the whole earth,
The dissatisfied people
Should discover their great worth.

DEAR LUCY

Thank you for your letter,
We are glad you are well,
To be very busy
The nicest thing to tell.

To like the work you do
Is the greatest asset,
Happy doing good work,
You will never regret.

The world demands so much
That young people can do,
High ideals do work well.
We are thankful for you.

Thank you for your letter,
Be sure to write again,
Share your garden of thoughts,
Like flowers in sun and rain.

BEAUTIFUL PLACE

Heaven is a beautiful place,
A lovely home for young and old,
Where all the gates are made of pearl
And all the streets are made of gold.

It is the city of the Lord,
Made for the people of God,
The Eternal City of Love,
Far above all the earthly sod.

God's children will always be there
Where angels sing around His throne,
And perfect peace will always reign
And no one will ever feel alone.

Heaven is a beautiful place,
A new Heaven and a New Earth,
Created by God's holy love.
The great miracle of the new birth.

BE THANKFUL

When people say do not,
They usually mean well,
No one should be angry
The truth they have to tell.

When people say do not,
It shows a deep concern,
There is danger ahead
In any way they turn.

When people say do not,
It is because they care
To try and help others,
Responsibility share.

When people say do not,
Be thankful it is so,
Someone is there to love,
Wherever they may go.

PRAYER

God does answer prayer
And gives the weary rest.
He knows each human need,
Supplies for them the best.

The burdens are heavy,
A rough and rugged road,
Bodies beg for mercy.
God will lighten the load.

Trials will disappear
And leave a better view,
The world will be brighter,
Better ways to pursue.

God does answer prayer,
And gives the weary rest,
A New Heaven and Earth,
The strength to meet each test.

LUCKY NO

It can be a lucky NO
Whenever you are in doubt,
It is better to be sure,
What the new world is about.

It can be a lucky NO
By taking the time to think
About the places broken
Then supply the missing link.

It can be a lucky NO,
Try better ways to secure,
Better things needed most,
A future to reassure.

It can be a lucky NO,
As the later years can tell,
To build a strong foundation,
To build a good building well.

RHYTHMIC BEAUTY

There is rhythmic beauty
In all the poets dreams,
The valleys and the mountains
Of Carroll County's streams.

Skies are always brighter
Above the brooks and springs,
Music is much sweeter
Where the mockingbird sings.

The rhododendron blooms
Close by flowing streams,
Shadows on the waters
Made by golden sunbeams.

There is rhythmic beauty
In each poetry line,
Heaven is much closer,
Common things more divine.

LONELY VALLEY

There is a lonely valley
Where the railroad used to be,
The train whistle loud and shrill,
Brought the children out to see.

There is a lonely valley
That history tries to keep,
Brave people who are gone
To rest in their long last sleep.

There is a lonely valley
That the children talk about,
The little schoolhouse is gone,
No children to sing and shout.

There is a lonely valley
Where the railroad used to be,
A dreamer would bring it back
For all the children to see.

SCREECH OWL

The screech owl's lonely cry
In the maple tree nearby,
Begging sounds, a lonely call,
When no one answers at all.

The screech owl's lonely cry
Sometimes moans, sometimes sigh,
Where are the friends, are they gone?
No neighbors stop, all pass on.

The screech owl's lonely cry,
The owl stays on tree trunks high.
There no footsteps on the ground,
Wandering dogs prowl around.

The screech owl's lonely cry,
No answers, it wonders why,
At last when the world is still,
It sleeps with the whippoorwill.

CROWS

Some people say the crow says caw,
It sounds more like maw and paw.
They answer back from the cornfield,
Fuss because the crops don't yield.

Some people say that crows say caw,
They only try to pick a flaw,
The worms they eat makes them good friends,
For some of their faults makes amends.

Some people say that crows say caw,
That crows are out to break a law,
Voices rough, they can friendly be,
Some of the crows good friends to see.

Some people say that crows say caw,
They only laugh and say hee haw.
The crow is gentle a good pet,
Loyally gives without regret.

LOVE ALONE

There is sadness on Christmas Day
With so many missing faces,
When the dear ones have gone away
To the far and distant places.

There is sadness on Christmas Day
When no Christmas bells are ringing.
No little children come to play,
No sweet voices come back singing.

There is sadness on Christmas Day
When memory brings it back clearly.
Lonely hearts are full of dismay,
Missing the ones we love dearly.

There is sadness on Christmas Day
With so many missing faces,
True love must search for them and pray,
For love alone somehow wins its way.

PRAY GOD TO PROTECT

Little unwed mother,
Her baby on her arm,
Listening to its heartbeat,
Protecting it from harm.

Little unwed mother,
The baby smiles and dreams,
Seeing all the angels,
A glimpse of heavenly gleams.

Little unwed mother
Dreams of another day,
When heaven seemed close,
But now so far away.

Little unwed mother,
Her baby on her arm,
We pray God to protect
And keep them safe from harm.

PRAY TO KEEP

I do not ask for Christmas gifts,
I pray to keep the things I have,
Family with love and fireside,
To face the future strong and brave.

I do not ask for Christmas gifts,
I pray for faith and strength to live
Above the evils of the world,
With willing hands to work and give.

I do not ask for Christmas gifts,
I pray for the desire to share,
The love of a generous heart,
A way of life love can prepare.

I do not ask for Christmas gifts,
I pray to keep the things I have,
To teach virtue, truth and honor,
A hungry world to try and save.

CAST AWAY

Self pity is an enemy,
Closes doors for the human mind,
The gates of opportunity
Will always be harder to find.

Self pity is an enemy
That will hide the morning sunrise,
Hide the glory of a new day
That always comes as a surprise.

Self pity is an enemy
That never recognizes friends,
It becomes too late to call them back,
To try again to make amends.

Self pity is an enemy
That happy hearts must cast away,
While praying for tomorrows,
Will make room for living today.

NEW YEAR'S GREETING

Happy New Year to all our friends,
We pray for peaceful days ahead,
We pray for strength and faith to work,
Give us this day our daily bread.

May there be strength and ideals high
To motivate each thought and deed,
To carry on all through the year,
Something to fill each human need.

New Years are always tomorrows,
The promise of something to last,
The hopes and dreams are ours to know,
From the memories of the past.

Happy New Year to all our friends,
May blessings come to young and old,
The happy sunrise for the young,
The golden sunsets for the old.

MERRY CHRISTMAS

A merry Christmas Day
Family and friends can meet,
To renew their friendships,
Their many friends to greet.

A merry Christmas day,
Remember and enjoy,
To make a better world,
The gift of time employ.

A merry Christmas Day
That memories hold dear,
That goes around the clock,
That will last through the year.

A merry Christmas Day,
Family and friends can meet,
Memories that live on
That time will help complete.

SHADOW MOUNTAIN

A place on Shadow Mountain
Where people dream wide awake
About all the tomorrows
When there will be no heartbreak.

A place on Shadow Mountain
Where there is sunshine and shade,
A land where dreams will come true
And memories never fade.

A place on Shadow Mountain,
Time its tapestries can weave.
Dreams become reality,
Are no longer make believe.

A place on Shadow Mountain
Where sunrise and sunsets stay,
On lovely Shadow Mountain
Where dreams never go away.

SUFFERING

Humans being what they are
Must all some suffering see.
Suffer for good or evil,
Which suffering shall it be?

To suffer for doing right
May hardship often be,
But happy changes will come,
Light eternal paths for thee.

Evil may look like treasure,
Where all its lights sometimes gleam,
But brings darkness in the end
Suffering without a sunbeam.

God trusted His children so much
They can roam the earth quite free.
Choose earth a little while,
Or heaven eternally.

GOOD-BYE

Good-bye, dear little tooth,
You were a friend to me,
Gone away forever,
No longer there to see.

Faithful through many years
And never did complain,
To vanish overnight
And can't come back again.

There is a vacant place,
As all the world can see,
And that one missing tooth
Had personality.

Good-bye, dear little tooth,
Thank you for memory,
That tells of useful lives,
Why they must always be.

FRIENDS

The kittens and the birds eat,
They share the same food from a dish,
In a friendly way they all know
The kittens and birds make a wish.

They know when a rain is coming,
They all come out when winds are still,
They know when cold winds will blow,
Hear it coming over the hill.

The little birds are all content,
The little kittens softly purr,
The world will become very still,
Before the wind begins to stir.

Kittens and starlings are good friends,
They are not enemies people see,
Friends that share a world together,
In peace they eat and all agree.

GOOD MOTHER

I saw a little cat,
She was washing her face,
Happy and content,
Motions were full of grace.

Along came the kittens,
Then she gave them a lick
With her soft velvet tongue,
She made they shiny slick.

Kittens were contented,
They all began to purr,
A happy family,
They belonged to her.

They all play together
And have no wish to spat,
Mother taught them better,
The good, nice mother cat.

WORTH MORE

Gentle voices, sweet smiles each day
Are worth more than gifts once a year,
Will bring much more happiness,
Create a world of love and cheer.

Gentle voices, sweet smiles each day,
Are worth more than silver and gold,
Than being kept for other days, wealth
No one knows it is there to hold.

Gentle voices, sweet smiles each day,
Arc something wonderful to own,
Then no one will be cast away,
To be unhappy and alone.

Gentle voices, sweet smiles each day,
Are like angel wings that enfold,
A glimpse of Heaven can be seen,
Riches and wealth to never be sold.

WHERE?

Where are the friendly people,
All the little girls and boys,
That liked to hear church bells ring,
That brought the world many joys?

Where are the friendly people,
All the good neighbors and friends,
With their friendly helping hands,
That in all their friendship blends?

Where are the friendly people,
Who their friendly vigils keep,
Are they in some distant land
Or have they all gone to sleep?

Where are the friendly people,
When will they come home to stay,
Be the lovely friends we know
In the old-fashioned way?

GIRLS AND BOYS

Little girls are sugar and spice,
Little boys are just as nice,
To look at them all clean and neat,
Makes all of life much more complete.

Little girls are sugar and spice
Two little girls are blessings twice,
Like roses that bloom, flowers sweet.
Their company is always a treat.

The little boys are just as nice
Three little boys are blessings thrice.
The little boys fine and strong
In happy homes where they belong.

Little girls are sugar and spice,
The little boys are just as nice,
Little children are gifts to love
Sweet treasures from Heaven above.

PEACE OF GOD

Let the peace of God rule in your hearts,
All speech be seasoned with grace and love,
That understanding never departs,
Continue in prayer to always move.

Admonish one another in psalms and hymns,
Put on the new peace behind the old,
The peace of Heaven that never dims,
Spiritual grave is worth more than gold.

Let no one despoil life through deceit,
Let no vanity carry you astray,
Or ever cause the soul to retreat,
Be ye complete in Christ, never stray.

Personal belief an anchor stone,
Risen with Christ through faith in His Word,
Where Christ in Glory reigns on His Throne,
His presence near He will be heard.

THE CHURCH

Is the Church a place to retreat,
Is it a place to testify,
Does the world see the Mercy Seat
Or place where the world passes by?

Do the little children around,
Know the Church as a happy place,
Or a place of forgotten ground,
Or a place to learn more of Grace?

Is it a witness to the world,
Where christian fellowship is sought,
The Word is taught, a precious pearl,
The glory of Heaven is taught.

Is the Church a place to retreat
Or a place that wants to reach out,
Makes the kingdom of Heaven complete
Where there is faith and never doubt?

STONE FENCE

A remnant of the stone fence stands,
That was once the campus pride,
Tall buildings stand on the lands,
No Founder's Hall by its side.

Trees are left above the wall,
One single flowering quince,
Most of the landmarks are gone,
With dreams vanished long since.

The stone fence was a symbol,
Of wisdom that would long last,
Of character, high ideals
Always be proud of the past.

A remnant of the stone fence stands,
That was once the campus pride,
May history keep records,
Good work cannot be denied.

PEACEFUL RELATIONS

There must be peaceful relations,
Between the people in the home,
That ties families together,
So children will not want to roam.

There must be peaceful relations,
The gentle ties of love and grace,
That will create much happiness,
That makes a home of any place.

There must be peaceful relations,
That will reach from the earth to sky,
That will soar on wings of love,
That will on peaceful ways rely.

There must be peaceful relations
That creates a world without fear,
That makes the world a lovely place,
Where hope and joy are always near.

MUCH TO DISCOVER

There is much to discover,
And so many things are nice,
That are like the lovely fruits,
That are flavored with spice.

There is much to discover,
Unseen beauty all around,
A little bit of searching,
Shows where beauty can be found.

There is much to discover,
That is like jewels and gold,
The hidden truths in a book,
A lovely world to unfold.

There is much to discover,
When people cease to be blind,
To a world of grace and love
That is trying to be kind.

EXPERIENCE

Experience is a teacher
Many people would like to change,
The hand of time leaves its imprint,
There is no way to rearrange.

Experience is a teacher
People do not know how to choose,
A few wise choices made each day,
There would be fewer things to lose.

Experience is a teacher,
Its value only time can tell,
When the past is brought back to view
And history says all is well.

Experience is a teacher
To appreciate and to see,
The little things we do today,
Rewarding tomorrows will be.

OIL IN THE LAMPS

Oil in the lamps ready to light,
To shine in the darkness through the night,
Oil in the lamps to make a glow,
To light the way people should go.

Oil in the lamps, their lights to give,
The faith to work, the faith to live,
Oil in the lamps their light to share,
A steady gleam is always there.

Oil in the lamps the world can see,
Faithfulness and humility,
Goodness and love, the right and just,
All life is a beautiful trust.

Oil in the lamps faithfully burn,
Keeps the road straight, shows where to turn,
Oil in the lamps, the west or east
Guests will go to the wedding feast.

ONLY THE TOMORROWS

Today is fleeting time,
Yesterday already past,
Only the tomorrows,
They will forever last,

Yesterdays cannot change,
Today is ours to live,
Tomorrow will be like
The today's gifts we give.

Accept the yesterdays
And profit from mistakes,
Remember honest love,
Never, never forsakes.

Today is fleeting time,
The threads of time are fast,
The knots we tie today
They will forever last.

THE WORLD NEEDS

The world needs cheerful people
That have optimistic views,
To bring a little sunshine,
And to chase away the blues.

All people have their troubles,
And they often feel alone,
Theer is a kindred spirit
In every cornerstone.

The world needs cheerful people
To create a happy chain,
To plant a garden of hope,
Bring flowers to earth again.

The world needs cheerful people
With an optimistic note,
To give best things all their time.
Willing their time to devote.

CHRISTMAS WISHES

May glad tidings and joy
Be yours this Christmas Day,
The Holy Spirit direct
In all you do and say.

May God bless you each day
And the ones you hold dear,
Prosperity be yours
Through all the coming year.

May there be years of peace
And happy homes to know,
Family and fireside
And blessings to bestow.

May glad tidings and joy,
Be yours this Christmas Day,
May love guide footsteps,
Prepare for you the Way.

LOVE

Old people can love children,
People will never think them bad,
The precious jewels of childhood
Are here to make the whole world glad.

The world is full of people,
Who need to be so very brave,
The dear precious souls around
Are precious jewels to save.

There is the sunshine and the rain,
The lovely forest trees that wave,
The blessings on the young and old,
Love reaches from cradle to grave.

Old people can love the children,
Their lives can most unselfish be,
Each step on the pathway of life
Leads to blessed eternity.

LOVE LIVES AGAIN

There is a missing face,
There is a vacant chair,
There is a lonely place,
A dear one is not there,

Memories of a smile,
A voice gentle and low,
Music a little while,
Soft footsteps long ago.

The quiet eventide,
The bright morning sunrise,
Love walked side by side,
Under the starry skies.

There is a missing face,
The little dove will call,
Somewhere love lives again to grace,
The evening shadows fall.

WHO

Who wants to go on strike,
And hurt a hungry child,
Destroy a world of peace,
Cause the world to go wild?

Who wants to go on strike,
Against the daily tasks,
And not to know the needs
Or hear the voice that asks?

Who wants to go on strike
With only self to see,
Forget other people,
The things that ought to be?

Who wants to go on strike?
There is a place to fill,
Love and thoughts for others,
In a world of good will.

CREATE

Create a little world,
That is nice clean and sweet,
Then put love into it,
It makes a world complete.

The people may be poor,
They cannot be too sad,
Love is the thing that works,
Makes a little world glad.

The ups and downs in life,
May find a rugged road,
But when love is there
It makes a lighter load.

Create a little world,
That makes a better way,
Tomorrow is better
To live and work this way.

PICK A FLOWER

Pick a flower or two
While searching for a dream,
Gather a few rosebuds
And a golden sunbeam.

See a shining pebble
In a sparkling stream,
There will be jewels
Like diamonds that gleam.

Look across the valley
Above the mountaintops,
With a rainbow promise
That never, never stops.

Pick a flower or two
While searching for a dream,
Moments of time will stitch
A lovely, lovely seam.

BE THANKFUL

Be thankful for today,
Hold fast to all the dreams,
Today may hold the best
For tomorrow's sunbeams.

Be thankful for today
And waste no time to fret.
Today may hold treasures
Too precious to forget.

Be thankful for today,
See the good not the bad,
All the little blessings
Will make tomorrow glad.

Be thankful for today,
It is accepted time.
For work we ought to do
To climb to heights sublime.

DISCIPLINE

Discipline is the word,
That describes self-control
Coordinates a life
And makes a happy soul.

Discipline smoothes the way
That otherwise is rough,
But it sustains a life
And that will be enough.

Discipline will create
A great desire to live,
Always think of others,
A fruitful life to give.

Discipline is the word
That describes self-control,
That heals a world of doubt,
That makes a good life whole.

GOD CAN SEE

Man proposes, God disposes,
And thus it will forever be.
For God can see through the ages,
What man is unable to see.

The world is torn and in chaos,
Man stumbles often, trys to find,
Yet God offers a helping hand,
Because that man is often blind.

Prayer could mend so many things,
God gave His promise to Redeem,
Man depends on self and cannot see,
God sends a light, a golden beam.

Man proposes, God disposes,
The answer is always the same.
Through Christ's redemption, redeeming love,
Peace will come through His holy name.

THE WIND

The wind is a good friend
That blows away the dust,
Leaves the air sweet and clean,
For the just and unjust.

The wind is a good friend
That brings clouds and the rain.
Then takes the clouds away,
The sun will shine again.

The wind is a good friend,
The little birds can tell,
How long to be quiet,
When all the world is well.

The wind is a good friend,
That blows away the dust,
The touch of God on earth,
That instills love and trust.

REAL RICHES

To gain the world and lose a soul,
A broken heart, nothing is left,
A world of gold cannot ease pain,
A heart that is sad, a soul bereft.

Bereft of love, quiet and peace,
No gentle touch to bring heart ease,
The quiet calm to understand
The little things that gently please.

A world of plenty in chaos,
Disappointed always and alone,
Looking for friendship good and true,
Love and family and hearthstone.

To gain the world and lose a soul,
Lonely for love and not for gold,
Cling to the touch of friendship and love,
Real love to cherish and hold.

DON'T BE A PESSIMIST

Don't be a pessimist
And spoil a lovely day,
Pessimistic people
Will often lead astray.

The same sun is shining,
On the good and the bad,
Some wear a happy smile,
Other people are sad.

Be a tower of strength,
Help other people face,
It can always be done
Through God's mercy and grace.

Don't be a pessimist
And spoil a lovely day,
God's throne is in Heaven,
There is another day.

NEW RIVER

New River swiftly flows
By New River Valley doors,
Water flows toward the sea,
While it a dreamland restores.

It flows into Kanowah,
Then into the Ohio,
The mighty Mississippi,
Then the Gulf of Mexico.

The murmur of its waters
Carries along mountain songs,
The sound of lowing cattle,
The little lamb that belongs.

The New River swiftly flows,
Begins with mountain springs,
The little people hear it
And love the songs it sings.

GOD SO LOVES

God so loves His children,
He will never forsake,
He holds the healing touch,
That heals grief and heartbreak.

He is always ready,
To hear and understand,
The child that will listen,
To God's loving command.

If ye love me then keep—
His commands are few,
Because that God loves you,
Then you will love Him too.

God so loves His children,
Prepares for them the way,
He gives them breath of life,
To worship and to pray.

LOVE

Love married a man years ago,
Where the man went, love does not know,
Love married a man years ago,
With a sweetheart's love to bestow.

Loving is still hoping, no regrets,
Troubles and trials often besets,
Looking for the moon, nothing mars
The dream of trying to reach stars.

Love goes on, forever alive,
Love never dies, will always thrive.
Angel wings on thoughts are still there,
Heavenly dreams are theirs to share.

Love married a man years ago,
Where the man went, love does not know,
The windows of Heaven are bright,
Love is waiting to say goodnight.

A CHRISTIAN'S PRAYER

A Christian should never doubt
That a prayer was not heard,
God is always listening
As promised in His Word.

Unselfish prayer for others,
All things happen for the best,
In hardship and trials of life,
There will be strength for each test.

Sufficient unto the day,
Will always be strength to live,
Remember and love others,
There is something good to give.

A Christian should never doubt,
The judgment of God is just,
And try to keep on living,
In Heavenly faith and trust.

PRAYER

Christians do not pray for ease,
Or to do just as they please,
They pray for the strength to share,
To help others, burdens bear.

They pray that their eyes may see,
The troubled places on earth,
Place value on souls of men,
Holy Spirit and new birth.

They are not afraid to tell,
The Gospel of the good news,
That salvation is for all,
God's love is for them, they can choose.

Christians do not pray for ease,
They pray they will understand,
Pray for a dying lost world
And offer a helping hand.

CHURCH

A church is a lonely place,
When the people go away,
Silence is in the darkness.
When there is no one to pray.

Where have all the people gone,
In the hedges or on the road,
With the burdens that they carry,
No place to relieve a load.

A church is a lonely place,
There is silence in the pews
The Holy Spirit gives strength,
With Holy Power that renews.

A church is a lonely place,
When the people go away,
Please, God, bring the people back,
Give them peace and grace to stay.

LONELY

The world is a lonely place
When the children are all gone
The sound of footsteps echo
While memory carries on.

There is the sound of music,
Little children are at play,
Now it seems a long, long time
It was only yesterday.

The shadows in the valleys
Beneath the stars in the skies,
Often bring back the morning,
Little children's smiling eyes.

The world is a lonely place
When the children are all gone,
Today's children must come home,
To comfort and carry on.

BE YE FRUITFUL

Be ye fruitful in good works,
And never discouraged be,
When the time comes for harvest,
The answer is there to see.

A work of the Lord,
Be strengthened with all might,
Give thanks unto the Father,
For glorious Eternal light.

Do not cease to pray always,
Filled with the knowledge and love,
Delivered from the darkness,
Holy guidance from above.

Trials of life will test faith,
Patience and suffering will see,
The answer, power of God,
Joyfulness eternity.

RHYTHM

Life is made of rhythm,
The beating heart at birth,
Will go on through life,
While a soul is on earth.

Life is made of rhythm,
That goes along with time,
Climbs to heights of Heaven.
To reach a life sublime.

Life is made of rhythm,
No deed is commonplace,
God's love will always bless,
With benefits and grace.

Life is made of rhythm,
The beating heart at birth,
All the things God creates
Man is of greatest worth.

HAPPY DAYS

Happy days are here again,
The children are home from school.
Family by the fireside,
While learning the Golden Rule.

The friendliness in the home,
All have a story to tell,
Then a quiet night of rest,
That all in their world is well.

All the plans for tomorrow,
And all the promises made,
They create a memory
Too precious to ever fade.

Happy days are here again,
Children remember the days,
Parents remember too
In more than a thousand ways.

UNSELFISH LOVE

Unselfish love like sunshine
Blesses earth after a rain,
Sees a happy good morning,
Rejoices in love again.

Unselfish love like sunshine
Rejoices in all the earth,
That counts all the little things
And is thankful for their birth.

Unselfish love like sunshine
Can always see sunsets glow,
Know that all the tomorrows
Will their blessings bestow.

Unselfish love like sunshine
Has the faith to look and see
That good work is never lost,
A gift for eternity.

TODAY

Today is the tomorrow
That we thought of yesterday,
And it is the only time
To make plans that will stay.

It is easy to plan
In faith and try to live,
Yesterdays are all gone,
Only today can give.

Today, accepted time,
So never be in haste,
It is a gift from God
No one should ever waste.

Today is the tomorrow
We lost on yesterday,
Thank God, this is the time
To plan a better day.

THANKSGIVING DAY

Time for inventory,
On this Thanksgiving Day,
Count the many blessings
That are coming my way.

Thank God for families,
The fellowship of friends,
Many good memories
With which Thanksgiving blends.

Good thoughts are a blessing,
With food and shelter too,
Families together
All rejoicing anew.

Time for Thanksgiving,
The family goes to church,
The Holy Spirit saves,
Always knows where to search.

ANOTHER DOOR

Open another door,
To see the other side,
And see all the good things,
That the Lord will provide.

The day may be dreary,
But let the sunshine in,
To clear away the dust
From the land Might Have Been.

The world will be brighter,
Something be there to cheer,
To bring another view,
For a happier year.

Open another door,
There may be something good,
The atmosphere may change,
Bring a happier mood.

MANTLE OF AGE

The mantle of age on our shoulders
Brings humility to weary heads,
Memory brings back our dreams again,
With its halo of gold around us spreads.

So many places that we have seen,
So many of our loved ones are gone,
They will always be alive and real,
As long as our memories live on.

The mantle of age on our shoulders
Can cover a precious golden store,
We can cherish all the lovely things
About our people gone before.

The mantle of age on our shoulders
Adds wisdom that is a golden store,
Jewels that bring joy to our souls,
A crown of peace to wear evermore.

CRUMBS

A few little crumbs of comfort
That we can scatter here and there,
Sometimes in later life we learn
They are the greatest things we share.

The few kind words that we say,
Words of comfort we know are right,
May help someone through long weary hours,
Give them rest in stillness of night.

A few little crumbs of comfort,
Can be expressed in many ways,
That may be kept within the heart,
That will help much in coming days.

THINK

It is better to think
Before taking a leap
Than finding out too late
That mistakes always keep.

It is better to think
About the work we do,
To keep on in the right road,
Then troubles will be few.

It is better to think,
Read the directions right,
See the bright new sunrise,
See the sun shining bright.

It is better to think
And make a clear outline,
Clear directions show
A good road is divine.

UNDERSTANDING

A little understanding
Of burdens that people bear,
Will bring a little sunshine
Into a life anywhere.

The darkness will disappear
Beneath the sunshine of love,
While an angel's wings whisper
To the angel wings above.

A little understanding,
Like the lovely flowers bloom,
Where the bluebirds in the morning
Can chase away all the gloom.

A little understanding
Will make a world that is new,
Little love stars shine again,
In lovely skies of blue.

AT HOME

I would rather be at home
Than any place that I know,
Though it is a humble place,
It has comfort to bestow.

I would rather be at home
And do the humble things,
In the quiet peace that comes,
The simple joy that it brings.

I would rather be at home
Where that love is by my side
Than have a million dollars
And know that love was denied.

I would rather be at home
And live in a simple way,
Where quiet and peace can come
And be so welcome to stay.

NO REGRETS

Young love has dreams it must fulfill,
Old love dreams of making its will.
Young love sees promise through the years,
Old love remembers joy and tears.

Young love has dreams that go on and on,
Old love has fears of being alone,
Young love can see that life is sweet,
Old love has often met defeat.

Young love has much of life to lend,
Old love has much that it should mend,
Young love has dreams of life, all nice,
Old love has found it pays a price.

Old love, young love should both be kind,
Then love rewards with peace of mind,
As love will give, love begets,
The heart rejoices, no regrets.

CRUMBS OF COMFORT

Little crumbs of comfort,
Sweet gentle words can be,
Or music of a song
That floated out to sea.

Little crumbs of comfort
Can be a happy smile,
Memories that return
After a weary mile.

Little crumbs of comfort
Can be the friendly hands,
Their ministry of love,
That always understands.

Little crumbs of comfort
Are around all the time,
To always look for them,
Makes life much more sublime.

GOD'S GLORY

The sunrise is beautiful,
The sunset is just as bright,
The beauty of the morning
Lingers in the sunset at night.

The long, busy day between,
When midday shadows fall,
Meadowlark in the meadow
Answers the mockingbird's call.

It is time for work and play,
In the busy world about,
The world's a beautiful place,
Thanks given without a doubt.

The sunrise is beautiful,
The sunset is just as bright,
The soul that knows God's glory
Will be happy in its flight.

I THANK GOD

I thank God for little children—
Small enough to trample on toes,
Their gentle touch brings the comfort,
Creates memories like a rose.

I thank God for little children—
They are small for such a short while.
Cherish the sound of their sweet voices,
Their tender touch and sweet smile.

I thank God for little children—
They all too soon will go away,
Memory is a golden store,
Creates good things for them each day.

I thank God for little children—
Remember compassion and love,
All the lovely things on earth,
Always reach to heaven above.

MUST BE

There must be someone who cares,
Then there is someone who shares,
The world is a needy place
For a feeble human race.

Little babies often born
In a world that is war-torn,
Need the tenderness and care,
To a better world prepare.

There should be a vision clear,
Tomorrows are always near,
Make the world a better place
That is full of love and grace.

There is someone who cares,
Then there is someone who shares,
For each day of time must be
A part of eternity.

TEARS OF LOVE

Jesus weeps with His children,
His tears are the tears of love,
His peace is there to comfort,
Heavenly peace from above.

Jesus weeps with His children
When they sail a troubled sea,
He holds out a helping hand,
Says, children, Come follow Me.

Jesus weeps with His children,
His pity and compassion show,
Love me keep my commandments,
Paths of peace and grace to show.

Jesus weeps with His children,
They will never alone be,
Jesus the same forever,
Says, children, come follow me.

GREATEST HONOR

The greatest honor to the dead
To keep their good work going on,
Honor them before all the world
When their presence on earth is gone.

The greatest honor to the dead
That records of history tell,
That high ideals are worth keeping,
Future foundations will be built well.

The greatest honor to the dead,
Cherish their work noble and fine,
Heaven will always be closer,
A good life be more divine.

The greatest honor to the dead,
Memories cherish and keep,
To keep their good work going,
For tomorrow we too shall sleep.

FRIENDSHIP IS A TWO-WAY STREET

Friendship is a two-way street.
That is made of give and take,
To be grateful for good gifts,
To forgive and not forsake.

Friendship is a two-way street,
Friendly people understand,
To keep a clear right of way,
To hold out a helping hand.

Friendship is a two-way street,
Helpful people come and go,
Love is kind, does not demand,
With its blessings to bestow.

Friendship is a two-way street,
That people must not forget,
With grace to give and receive,
Thanks given without regret.

ALL THINGS

All things work together for good
For the people who love the Lord,
Called according to His purpose,
That trust in God's Most Holy Word.

The sorrows and grief that break hearts,
Sometimes no one can understand,
The years show the reason why,
That troubles all their tolls demand.

The years will bring battle and strife,
There is a question, what is best,
Then later years will bring to view,
Each day of life another test.

All things work together for good,
A Christian must always believe,
The faith to work, live and believe,
With many blessings to receive.

GOOD HABITS

Good habits are good friends
When there is work to do,
A steady way of work,
It will soon carry through.

Good habits are good friends,
And they will always be
The helping hand of love
For all the world to see.

Good habits are good friends,
Blessed are ones who know
The world's a better place,
With blessings to bestow.

Good habits are good friends,
Stories tomorrows tell,
Because of good habits,
Tomorrow will be well.

STEWARDSHIP OF SORROW

There is a channel of blessing,
Through the stewardship of sorrow,
To tell the world about Heaven
A glorious home tomorrow.

The Holy Spirit directs Christians
To try and win lost people,
The Lord will be in any house,
Where love of God is the steeple.

Suffering makes ties of kinship,
Where the glory of God is reigning,
The possibility of souls,
The Holy Spirit is gaining.

There is a blessing in the grief,
To win the lost by believing,
The love of God is always there,
God's children are receiving.